Clues in Corpses

A Closer Look at Body Farms

By Sophie Washburne

Portions of this book originally appeared in
Body Farms by Diane Yancey.

LUCENT
PRESS

Published in 2018 by
Lucent Press, an Imprint of Greenhaven Publishing, LLC
353 3rd Avenue
Suite 255
New York, NY 10010

Designer: Deanna Paternostro
Editor: Jennifer Lomardo

Cataloging-in-Publication Data

Names: Washburne, Sophie.
Title: Clues in corpses: a closer look at body farms / Sophie Washburne.
Description: New York : Lucent Press, 2018. | Series: Crime Scene Investigations | Includes index.
Identifiers: ISBN 9781534562714 (pbk.) | ISBN 9781534561724 (library bound) | ISBN 9781534562318 (ebook)
Subjects: LCSH: Human decomposition–Research–Tennessee–Juvenile literature. | Human skeleton–Analysis–Juvenile literature. | Forensic osteology–Tennessee–Juvenile literature. | Crime laboratories–Tennessee–Juvenile literature. | Forensic anthropology–United States–Juvenile literature.
Classification: LCC QP87.W37 2018 | DDC 599.9–dc23

Printed in the United States of America

CPSIA compliance information: Batch #CW18KL: For further information contact Greenhaven Publishing LLC, New York, New York at 1-844-317-7404.

Please visit our website, www.greenhavenpublishing.com. For a free color catalog of all our high-quality books, call toll free 1-844-317-7404 or fax 1-844-317-7405.

Contents

Foreword

For decades, popular television programs and movies have depicted the life and work of police officers, detectives, and crime scene investigators. Many of these shows and films portray forensic scientists as the brains responsible for cracking cases and bringing criminals to justice. Undoubtedly, these crime scene analysts are an important part in the process of crime solving. With modern technology and advances in forensic analysis, these highly trained experts are a crucial component of law enforcement systems all across the world.

Police officers and detectives are also integral members of the law enforcement team. They are the ones who respond to 911 calls about crime, collect physical evidence, and use their high level of training to identify suspects and culprits. They work right alongside forensic investigators to figure out the mysteries behind why a crime is committed, and the entire team cooperates to gather enough evidence to convict someone in a court of law.

Ever since the first laws were recorded, crime scene investigation has been handled in roughly the same way. An authority is informed that a crime has been committed; someone looks around the crime scene and interviews potential witnesses; suspects are identified based on evidence and testimony; and, finally, someone is formally accused of committing a crime. This basic plan is generally effective, and criminals are often caught and brought to justice. Throughout history, however, certain limitations have sometimes prevented authorities from finding out who was responsible for a crime.

There are many reasons why a crime goes unsolved: Maybe a dead body was found too late, evidence was tampered with, or witnesses lied. Sometimes, even the greatest technology of the age is simply not good enough to process and analyze the evidence at a crime scene. In the United States during the 20th century, for example, the person responsible for the infamous Zodiac killings was never found, despite the earnest efforts of hundreds of policemen, detectives, and forensic analysts.

In modern times, science and technology are integral to the investigative process. From DNA analysis to high-definition surveillance video, it has become much more difficult to commit a crime and get away with it. Using advanced computers and immense databases, microscopic skin cells from a crime scene can be collected and then analyzed by a forensic scientist, leading detectives to the home of the culprit of a crime. Dozens of people work behind the scenes of criminal investigations to figure out the unique and complex elements of a crime. Although this process is still time-consuming and complicated, technology is constantly improving and adapting to the needs of police forces worldwide.

This series is designed to help young readers understand the systems in place to allow forensic professionals to do their jobs. Covering a wide range of topics, from the assassination of President John F. Kennedy to 21st-century cyber-criminals, these titles describe in detail the ways in which technology and criminal investigations have evolved over more than 50 years. They cite eye-witnesses and experts in order to give a detailed and nuanced picture of the difficult task of rooting out criminals. Although television shows and movies add drama to the crime scene investigation process, these real-life stories have enough drama on their own. This series sticks to the facts surrounding some of the highest-profile criminal cases of the modern era and the people who work to solve them and other crimes every day.

Introduction
Creepy or Cool?

When people hear the words "body farm," their first reaction may be confusion. Body farms are not talked about much, so people may not know what they are. Some people think they are places where murderers bury their victims' bodies; others think they exist so organs can be harvested; still others think they are locations where victims are lured to be murdered. When people find out what body farms actually are, they are generally either disgusted or interested to learn more.

Body farms are research facilities where forensic experts study bodies to learn how they decompose, or break down, under different circumstances. Forensics is the use of science in crime-solving; according to the College of American Pathologists, forensic scientists "are experts in investigating and evaluating cases of sudden, unexpected, suspicious and violent death, as well as other specific classes of death defined by state laws."[1] However, to understand the results of their investigations, forensic scientists must be familiar with the ways bodies decompose, which is why body farms are important.

Fear and Outrage

There are several reasons why people may disapprove of body farms. One reason is some people feel it is not respectful to the bodies or to the people who may accidentally see them. For example, when a young man in Knoxville, Tennessee, found a body decomposing near the site where he and his coworkers were laying out boundaries for a new parking lot in 1985, he was shocked and disgusted. That night, he told his mother about his unpleasant experience. She, too, was shocked and, being a leader of a local advocacy group called Solutions to Issues of Concern to Knoxvillians (S.I.C.K.), decided to take action. Within days, members of S.I.C.K. rallied to voice their disapproval, holding a demonstration outside the facility at the University of Tennessee Medical Center and carrying signs that read, "This Makes Us S.I.C.K."[2] The group was especially indignant that such experiments were being carried out in plain view of the general population.

Anthropology professor Bill Bass, the head of the body farm, met with the protesters and explained that the facility was not designed to shock or offend, but to carry out groundbreaking work that would help law enforcement solve murders. The bodies were closely watched over and treated with respect, and the bones were carefully stored when the experiments were complete. The crisis passed, but the professor realized that the chain-link fence around the facility was not a good enough barrier. Shortly thereafter, a wooden privacy fence was also built inside the chain-link enclosure, discouraging curious people and protecting unwitting passersby from disturbing sights.

Another reason people protest body farms is that they do not want one near where they live. For instance, in May 2014, Fox Valley Technical College in Wisconsin proposed creating a body farm so researchers could study the effects of cold weather on bodies.

Forensic anthropologist Bill Bass, shown here inspecting a decomposing body, founded the world's first body farm.

However, people who lived near the college protested; they were worried they would be able to smell or see the bodies. The chairman of the college's Forensic Science Department assured them that a 10-foot (3 m) fence would keep people from seeing the bodies, and the cold weather would stop them from smelling anything. However, due to the neighbors' concerns, the project was never completed.

Interest and Respect

The term "body farm" gained the public's attention in 1993, when bestselling novelist Patricia Cornwell went to the Knoxville research site for a visit and wrote about a "decay research facility" in her fifth novel, a thriller titled *The Body Farm*. "Patricia says she didn't coin that term," Bass said. "[She] went to a lecture at the FBI Academy, and one of [the agents], Irving Futrell comes in and says, 'I've just gotten back from the Body Farm.' And she wrote that down for her book. So, I think it was coined by an FBI agent and used in a meeting at the FBI Academy and picked up by Patricia Cornwell."[3] In the years that followed, body farms gained the respect of the scientific community as sites of some of the most important developments ever to be made in forensic science.

The Knoxville facility eventually became the Anthropology Research Facility (ARF). The center includes the body farm, skeletal collections, and a computer data bank of skeletal measurements and other information. Studies done there continue to provide new insights into human death and decomposition. Forensic experts, law enforcement officials, and the public have become more accepting of human decomposition research, and other body farms have been established. As of 2017, there are seven body farms in the United States. In addition to the one in Tennessee, there are two in Texas and one each in Colorado, North Carolina, Florida, and Pennsylvania. The only body farm outside the United States is the Australian Facility for Taphonomic Experimental Research (AFTER), which opened in 2016.

Because the body farms are in different areas, each has a slightly different focus. In Texas, for example, they focus on decomposition issues unique to Texas and other western states. One issue there that is more of a problem than in other areas is the presence of vultures. Being able to recognize beak marks, scratch marks, and dung deposits on a decayed corpse is vital in Texas. Texas State anthropology professor Michelle Hamilton said, "This is the kind of information we need to get in the hands of law enforcement and other anthropologists, to say things are different in different areas."[4]

Researchers   at   body   farms

Author Patricia Cornwell (shown here) made the term "body farm" popular.

continually look for new and better ways to determine the post-mortem interval (PMI)—the time between death and the discovery of a body. They also work to find new ways to identify badly decomposed remains and to locate bodies hidden by murderers. With enthusiasm and determination, they believe no project is too unusual and no effort too great if it produces valid information. Their thirst for knowledge causes them to view errors and setbacks as motivation to try new things.

Bass's own story is a perfect example of their point of view. After a humiliating mistake that made him a laughingstock and haunted him for decades, the professor took the episode and made it a jumping-off point for a new life project. "Personally, I was embarrassed; scientifically, I was intrigued; above all, I was determined to do something about it,"[5] he recalled in his book *Death's Acre*, which he wrote with journalist and documentary filmmaker Jon Jefferson. How Bass's mistake triggered new advances in criminal investigation is the story of how the first body farm was created.

Chapter One
Learning from a Mistake

Some of the most important advancements in science and medicine have happened as a result of a mistake. For instance, penicillin, a powerful antibiotic that cures many diseases, was discovered when scientist Alexander Fleming threw away a petri dish full of bacteria that had become contaminated. The discarded petri dish grew mold that dissolved the bacteria, and Fleming realized he could use the mold to create medicine.

The best scientists learn from their mistakes and never give up; they see failure as a way to improve. This is exactly how Bill Bass ended up creating the world's first body farm and changing the field of forensics forever.

Uncovering the Body

In December 1977, Bass got a telephone call from a Tennessee county sheriff's department, asking him to investigate an apparent murder in the small town of Franklin, Tennessee.

Bass was Tennessee's state forensic anthropologist, a consultant with the Tennessee Bureau of Investigation, and head of the Anthropology Department at the University of Tennessee at Knoxville. A forensic anthropologist is a specialist who uses the human skeleton to answer questions of identity and trauma in medical and criminal cases. Because of his position and expertise, Bass was the person who law enforcement called when a badly decayed corpse needed to be examined.

Upon arrival in Franklin, Bass learned that the body in question had been found in a private family cemetery on the grounds of a historic Tennessee estate. The estate was owned by Ben and Mary Griffith, a doctor and his wife, but it had originally belonged to the Shy family, eight members of whom were buried in the cemetery. Mary Griffith had called the police when she noticed that the grave of Civil War veteran Lieutenant Colonel

A gravesite such as this one was a familiar site for Bill Bass. Police called Bass to investigate the headless corpse they found buried in William Shy's grave.

Occupation: Forensic Anthropologist

Job Description:
Forensic anthropologists help identify unknown bodies or body parts and skeletal remains. They also help determine the estimated time since death and cause of death. Work is carried out both in the lab and in the field. The work involves exposure to potentially dangerous and disturbing situations.

Education:
Aspiring forensic anthropologists must first earn either a bachelor of arts degree (BA) or a bachelor of science degree (BS) in anthropology from a four-year college. According to Binghamton University in New York State, a BS degree focuses more on the science that is relevant to a career in forensics. After getting a bachelor's degree, the student can then get a master of arts (MA) degree in anthropology, a doctor of philosophy (PhD) degree in anthropology, or both. To be accepted into the PhD program at Knoxville, an applicant must have either a BA or MA in anthropology or a minor in anthropology and a BS in a field such as biology or history. Other programs may have different requirements. Once their education is completed, forensic anthropologists may apply for board certification by the American Board of Forensic Anthropology.

Qualifications:
Aspiring forensic anthropologists must be objective, be persistent, and enjoy solving puzzles. They must be able to handle situations involving death and decay.

Salary:
$31,000 to $89,000 per year

William Shy had been disturbed. The grass had been removed from the plot, and a 3-foot (1 m) hole had been dug. Deputies first assumed that vandals had been searching for Civil War artifacts, such as swords and medals. That notion vanished, however, when they saw a headless corpse, barely covered with freshly turned earth, lying on top of the original coffin. It seemed logical to assume a murder victim had been dumped in Shy's grave.

Bass had retrieved plenty of bodies from graves in his career as a forensic anthropologist. During the 1950s, he had carried out archaeological work for the Smithsonian Institution, excavating (digging up) and analyzing Native American remains in South Dakota. He had been mentored by well-known anthropologist Charles E. Snow, who took him out on his first forensic case, and by Wilton Krogman, an internationally admired "bone detective." (The term forensic anthropologist was not recognized by the scientific community until 1972.) Thus, Bass was confident in his skills as he joined law enforcement officials who were gathered in the rain, eyeing the corpse that lay mostly covered with muddy earth.

The murder had obviously taken place some time before; a strong odor of decay told everyone that the victim was decomposing. Unbothered by the smell, Bass laid out a piece of plywood on which to place the body, then began carefully removing the dirt. As the hole got deeper, he climbed down inside with his feet on either side of the corpse so he could fully uncover it. "Counting my excavations of Indian burials in the Great Plains, I've been in somewhere around five thousand graves," he recalled. "By the time I die I suspect I'll hold some sort of unofficial record: 'body that's been in and out of the most graves ever.'"[6]

Taking a Guess

Once the body was uncovered, Bass saw that it had decayed to the point that the legs were separated from the pelvis and the arms were detached from the shoulders. Carefully, he handed the remains to deputies who placed them in anatomical order to resemble a complete body. When Bass was finished, the entire corpse—except for the head—was laid out before them. Despite the dirt, everyone could see that it was dressed in a formal black suit, black vest, pleated white shirt, and dress shoes. Bass remembered, "I wondered if the victim had been a waiter from some fancy Nashville or Franklin restaurant. Either that or a groomsman at a wedding."[7]

Part of the coffin lid had broken inward, so Bass peered inside the hole to see if the skull had fallen inside, but it was not there; he also noted that nothing was left of the late colonel Shy—all that was in the bottom of the coffin was a small amount of goo. He was not surprised—bodies rotted away quickly in Tennessee's damp earth, and Colonel Shy had been in the ground more than 100 years.

With the retrieval complete, Bass placed the remains in bags and put them in the trunk of his car. He planned to analyze them in his lab in Knoxville over the next few days. Deputies were anxious to get an estimate of time of death in order to begin their investigation, however, so he made a quick assessment. He looked at the still-pink tissue and remains of organs in the body cavity and stated, "It appears the man has been dead two months to a year ... A year may be a little too much."[8] The story of the discovery soon made the news,

An Unexpected Career Change

Bill Bass had no intention of becoming a forensic anthropologist until a chance incident in 1955 changed his life forever. He described the moment during an interview with HarperCollins publishers:

> *I was in graduate school at the University of Kentucky ... working on a master's degree in counseling. Just for fun, I was also taking a course in anthropology, and one day my anthropology professor, Dr. Charlie Snow, asked if I wanted to go with him on an identification case. Dr. Snow was a well known "bone detective," as forensic anthropologists were called back then, and he'd been asked to identify the burned body of a woman who was killed in a fiery head-on collision. While we were out there in the field that day, I had one of those life-changing "aha" moments, and the next week, I switched from counseling to anthropology. Besides changing the course of my life, that's the only case that's ever made me throw up!*[1]

1. Quoted in "Author Interview: Dr. Bill Bass on *Beyond the Body Farm*," HarperCollins. www.harpercollins.com/author/authorExtra.aspx?authorID=32695&isbn13=9780060875299&displayType=bookinterview.

and Bass's estimate was printed in the *Nashville Banner*, along with a quote from deputy Fleming Williams, who said, "It looks like we have a homicide on our hands."[9]

By the Numbers

1981

year the first body farm officially opened

Studying the Remains

Over the next few days, Bass studied the body more closely. The bones told him that he was looking at a young male in his mid-20s, between 5 feet 9 inches (1.7 m) and 6 feet (1.8 m) tall. Days later, the sheriff's deputy showed up with the missing skull—they had further searched the coffin and found the skull inside. The skull's shattered condition made it clear that he had been killed by a very large projectile. "Our mystery man had died a violent, instantaneous death,"[10] Bass decided.

While those clues were easy for

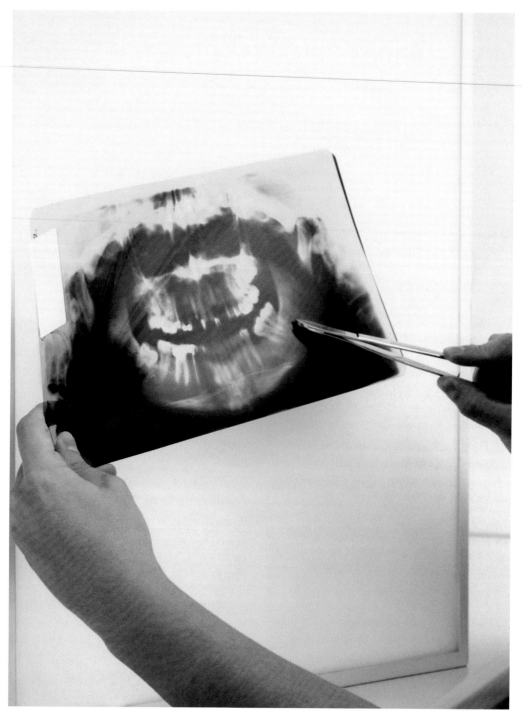

Teeth often provide forensic experts with clues.

the forensic expert to explain, others were more puzzling. Following standard procedures, Bass had simmered the remains in a pot of water to soften and remove the tissue from the bones. Oddly, the simmering remains gave off a chemical smell, rather than the stench of cooked flesh, indicating that the body had been embalmed—preserved with chemicals to prevent decay. Bass knew of no murderers who ever took the time to do that. In addition, although the victim had been well dressed, his teeth had many cavities, and one showed signs of an abscess, or infection. The lack of dental work in an apparently well-off man was also odd. The conflicting evidence made Bass uneasy. He started to wonder if the case was really a modern-day murder as everyone had first assumed.

A phone call from a confused crime technician added to his unease. The labels in the dead man's clothing could not be traced to any known manufacturer. The fibers were all natural—cotton and silk—and the lacing up the trouser legs was unique, as if it came from a different era. The man's shoes were unique, too. The technician finally asked if the body could be that of Lieutenant Colonel Shy, and Bass had to face his doubts head on.

As embarrassing as it was to admit, it made sense that the body was that of Shy. Dentists had not known how to do as much in the 1800s as they do today. Embalming was not common at that time, but a wealthy family like the Shys would have been able to afford it. They would have buried the lieutenant colonel in his best clothes, too, and would also have been able to afford the top-of-the-line, well-sealed coffin that lay in the grave. Made of cast iron mixed with lead, it had protected the body from moisture, and the lead had acted as a preservative. That explained the still-pink flesh on Shy's bones.

A quick check with local historians confirmed that William Shy had been 26 when he died. He had been killed by a large, soft bullet called a minié ball in the Battle of Nashville in 1864. The ball had traveled in a downward arc, striking Shy's skull from above so forcefully that it had fractured it into 17 pieces. The mystery of the headless corpse was solved: Shy had been pulled out of his coffin by grave robbers and reburied on top of it rather than inside it.

More to Learn

When local newspapers learned of Bass's inaccurate analysis, they quickly called him with questions. Specifically, they wanted to know how he had mistaken a Civil War corpse for a recent murder victim. Bass explained that the body had been exceptionally well

Autopsies gave forensic scientists some idea of the changes that take place after death, but more information about the process of decomposition was needed. This led to the creation of the first body farm.

preserved. It had also looked like it had been dumped into the grave, not pulled out of a hole in the top of the coffin. Taking the two circumstances together, he and the deputies had assumed they were looking at a recent murder victim. "I got the age, sex, race, height and weight right," he told a reporter from the *Nashville Banner*. "But I was off on the time of death by 113 years."[11]

The incident was printed in newspapers worldwide. Readers learned that one of the most respected forensic specialists in the United States had made a stupendous error. They wondered why he had not known better. Bass was embarrassed, but he was asking himself the same thing. He had had a fine education and a great deal of experience working with human remains. He was considered an expert by his scientific peers and by law enforcement officials. However, his miscalculation made it obvious that he knew too little about human decomposition, and that was because there was little mention of it in academic literature. Scientists had studied animal decomposition, and forensic pathologists had documented changes such as rigor mortis (stiffening of the body), algor mortis (decline in body temperature), and livor mortis (discoloring of parts of the body) that occurred in humans

in the hours immediately after death. However, the process of human decay had never been studied from beginning to end, mainly because social customs and religious beliefs had discouraged research.

Bass realized that if any good were to come from his blunder, he would have to break taboos and tackle the subject himself. Over the next few months, he formulated a plan. He would study human corpses in-depth in order to be better able to determine the PMI.

PMI is important because if time of death is known, police are better able to know the period of time they should be investigating, whether that is just a few days or many years in the past. Knowing time of death could also help police trace a victim's last movements, discover the last people to see them alive, and identify possible suspects.

By the Numbers

8

number of body farms in the world as of 2017

A Groundbreaking Facility

As head of the Department of Anthropology at the University of Tennessee, Bass was in a good position to tackle human decomposition research. He had several faculty members working in his department, and graduate students were willing and able to help carry out the projects he planned. He remembered,

> We had ... resources to do something that had never been done before: to establish a research facility unlike any other in the world—a research facility that would systematically study human bodies by the dozens, ultimately by the hundreds; a laboratory where nature would be allowed to take its course with mortal flesh, under a variety of experimental conditions. At every step, scientists and graduate students would observe the processes ... and chart the timing of human decomposition.[12]

Despite his new resolve, Bass was not sure he would be able to convince the university to support his efforts. He and *Death's Acre* coauthor Jon Jefferson explained, "The idea was simple; the implications—and the possible complications—were profound. By most cultural standards and values, such research could appear gruesome, disrespectful, even shocking."[13] His enthusiasm and vision were infectious and convincing, however. Jefferson said, "The thing about Dr. Bass that's so great is that he's able to take this macabre [shocking] subject and get you so fascinated ... You get caught up in his view that this is a scientific puzzle, an effort to uncover the truth. Ultimately, it's a quest for justice."[14]

University chancellor Jack Reese felt the same. He did not question the wisdom of the project and offered Bass a small plot of unused land behind the university's medical center as a work site. The land was not prime real estate—the hospital's trash had been dumped there until environmental regulations put an end to outdoor burning. However, Bass was satisfied.

The First Body

With land and a vision, Bass began his project in 1980. Neither he nor his students were skilled laborers, but they cut back the brush in the middle of the site, hauled in gravel, smoothed it, and then poured a 16-square-foot (1.5 sq m) slab of concrete. On the back of the slab, they built a small shed where they could store tools, instruments, and supplies such as shovels, scalpels, and latex

When Did They Die?

The post-mortem interval (PMI) is the period of time between death and discovery of the body. A number of medical and scientific techniques, based on changes that occur to the body, can be used to determine the PMI. Some of those changes include:

- *algor mortis*: A steady decline in body temperature that begins immediately after death and continues until body temperature matches air temperature, generally within two hours. How fast the temperature declines depends on factors such as the victim's body weight, the environment, and any coverings around and on the body, such as clothing.
- *rigor mortis*: A chemical change in the muscles after death resulting in a stiffening of the arms and legs. It can be used to determine the PMI until stiffening passes, generally in about 36 hours.
- *livor mortis*: Discoloration caused by the settling or pooling of blood into portions of the body closest to the ground after the heart stops circulating blood throughout the body. It can be used to help determine PMI up to 12 hours after death.
- *vitreous humor*: The clear gel that fills the space between the lens and the retina of the eyeball. It dries out after death. This happens fairly quickly, so it can be used to determine the PMI only in the early stages of death.
- *decomposition*: Predictable changes in the body that start almost immediately after death and last up to a year. Identifying a corpse's stage of decomposition can allow the PMI to be determined within a range of several hours.

gloves. The front part of the slab was left exposed so they could lay out the bodies they would study. Around the slab they ran a chain-link fence with a locked gate. They also ran electricity and water lines from the medical center and built a gravel driveway for delivery trucks to come and go. Bass and Jefferson pointed out, "People who know about the Body Farm today seem to think it sprang into existence fully formed, but that's not the way it happened at all. It came from humble beginnings, and it progressed by small steps."[15]

While the site was being prepared, Bass sent out letters of inquiry to medical examiners and funeral directors throughout Tennessee, asking for corpses for his experiment. Responses were slow, but one body was donated in May 1981. Bass drove his covered pickup truck to the Burris Funeral Home in Crossville, Tennessee, one hour west of Knoxville. A woman had agreed to donate the body of her 73-year-old father who had died of alcoholism, emphysema, and heart disease.

Bass had already decided that the identity of all his subjects would remain secret. To ensure that, he adopted a simple but unique identification code. The first donation of 1981 was known as 1-81. The second to arrive in 1981 would be 2-81 and so forth. Bass and his students respectfully placed 1-81 on the concrete pad they had built, took several photos, and covered him with a wire mesh cage to keep away rodents and other predators. Bass and Jefferson wrote of that moment, "death's acre was open for business. The Body Farm was born."[16]

Funny Name, Serious Work

The term "body farm" offended some serious researchers who saw it as inaccurate and unserious. It ignited the public's fancy, however, and became an established term for the facility and others like it.

After Patricia Cornwell published *The Body Farm*, the research facility caught the attention of the general public. With publicity came calls from everyone—from international journalists to Cub Scout den mothers—asking for a tour. Bass did not accept many requests because he believed that it would not be appropriate for the curious to wander among the bodies, staring and

The Knoxville body farm aimed to protect the anonymity of its subjects.

taking pictures. "This is a research facility with which we're trying to help police, morticians and society. It's not a tourist attraction,"[17] he pointed out.

As a research facility, the body farm in Tennessee soon became a respected learning institution, where the most dedicated scientists came to study. New body farms are held in similar high esteem. Those who are accepted are well aware of the unique opportunity they have been given. "I packed up or sold everything I had … to study under Dr. Bass. He's got an international reputation,"[18] said Emily Craig, who went on to become a forensic anthropologist for the Kentucky Medical Examiner's Office after studying at the Knoxville body farm.

Although prestigious, the small, messy plots of ground where the work is carried out are a far cry from the sterile, well-equipped rooms that ordinarily come to mind when the word laboratory is mentioned. By definition, body farms are insect infested, foul smelling, grim, and disturbing. Nevertheless, they are some of the most fascinating scientific establishments in the world.

Chapter Two
Inside the Body Farms

It was not long before Bass's body farm showed other forensic experts that it would be a good idea to create more body farms. Having them in multiple areas of the United States would help experts study decomposition under different conditions. For example, the weather conditions in Texas are much drier than those in Tennessee, so bodies decompose in different ways and at different rates in those two states. "The goal of law enforcement and the criminal justice system is to take … offenders off the street," said forensic expert Jason Byrd. "You can't expect [them] to do that without the proper tools."[19]

Originally, Bass hoped one body farm would be established in every state to give researchers a wide variety of decomposition data. However, as of 2017, there are still only seven in the United States. This is generally due to opposition from people who would have to live near the facility.

Fighting the Body Farms

Although supporters see body farms as important to society and law enforcement, most proposals to create more body farms are rejected for a variety of reasons. First, many people do not like to think about death and dying. Additionally, many are horrified at the thought of bodies being treated disrespectfully. For religious and moral reasons, they object to leaving a body in the open air where it could be torn apart and eaten by insects and animals.

In addition to being perceived as disrespectful, body farms are also perceived by some as unnecessary luxuries. The research is not judged to be worth the several million dollars it takes to start a body farm. In Nevada, a proposed facility near Las Vegas was not built because neither government nor university officials would come up with money to equip it. Forensic experts had cited its importance not only for law enforcement but also because the

Many people do not like the idea of vultures and other animals possibly eating human corpses.

Objection to Outsiders

NIMBY is an acronym for "not in my backyard." It describes the outrage and opposition expressed by members of a community when they learn that something they do not want, such as a landfill or a body farm, has been proposed for their neighborhood. In the following excerpt from the article "NIMBY," author Peter M. Sandman explained the basis of a community's outrage:

> Imagine pulling into your driveway after a long day's work and noticing that there are strangers picnicking in your back yard. "Get out of my back yard!" you demand. "Why?" they inquire. "We've done a site analysis. Your back yard is a prime location for our picnic. And we've done a risk assessment. Our picnic is unlikely to do any significant permanent damage to your back yard." They didn't ask your permission; they didn't invite you to the picnic; they won't even tell you exactly what they're eating. Odds are you're pretty steamed. Even if they're right about the substantive issues, even if you realize the risk to your back yard is actually minimal, you're still pretty steamed.

> Of course in this example it's literally your back yard. You have a legal right to forbid trespassing on your property. The principle is slightly different when it's not quite your back yard; it's the developer's property but your neighborhood, your community. But the feeling of being invaded by outsiders is much the same.[1]

1. Peter M. Sandman, "NIMBY," SAGE, February 17, 2008. www.psandman.com/col/nimby.htm.

climate and terrain is similar to that of the Middle East. By studying death in Nevada, researchers hoped to better understand death in places such as Iraq and Afghanistan. Michael Murphy, the former coroner of Clark County, Nevada, thinks the facility will be created one day. "I'm the eternal optimist," he said. "I believe there is a very strong possibility that it could happen. That it will happen."[20]

Finally, there are people who acknowledge the value of body farms, but do not want one in their neighborhood. For instance, Chico State University administrators discouraged efforts by anthropology professor Turhon Murad and others to create one in northern California, arguing that there was no appropriate location for one in their urban community. In Youngstown, Ohio, university administrators rejected a proposal made by the Ohio Bureau of Criminal Identification and Investigation after more than 150 people turned out to protest, citing possible health risks and declining property values. Former dean John Yemma stated, "We will not move forward with any plans without the full support of the residents of the area."[21]

Overcoming Objections

Planners faced public complaints when they first chose a location for Western Carolina University's body farm, so they downplayed their second choice in hopes of avoiding further objections. In a letter to nearby landowners, the facility was called a "forensics research station" and no mention was made of the corpses that would be decaying there. Residents soon guessed the truth, however, and again complained. "I'm wondering how half a dozen bodies strewn about land near my house would benefit me in the long run? I think I'd rather have a nice new landfill … down the road from my [house],"[22] wrote journalist Susan Reinhardt.

Planners at Texas State University in San Marcos, Texas, also had to overcome objections before they could set up their body farm. Their first proposed site was near a mall and drew protests from area residents who feared the odor from the facility would ruin their shopping spaces. The next proposed site, which was near an airport, caused airport officials to worry that vultures circling over the facility would get sucked into the engines of jets taking off or landing and cause crashes.

In some cases, though, residents support building new body farms. For instance, in 2017, when the Pasco County Sheriff's Office teamed up with the Florida Institute of Forensic Anthropology and Applied Sciences at the University of South Florida to announce the creation of a new body farm and law enforcement training facility, they received nothing but support from Pasco County residents. According to the *Tampa Bay Times*, "The project has been in the works for more than a year, since a smaller plan to locate a 'body farm' on county property in eastern Hillsborough was withdrawn after residents who lived near the proposed site protested. Officials have seen no such protest in Pasco."[23]

It is uncertain why some communities support body farms while others oppose them. One explanation may be because of the increased publicity they have gotten over the years; more people are aware of the important contributions body farms have made to forensic science. It may also be because of the popularity of television shows such as *CSI*, *NCIS*, *Bones*, and *Dexter*, which all feature forensic scientists.

When the Australian Facility for Taphonomic Experimental Research (AFTER) was proposed, professor Shari Forbes, the head of the facility, gave speeches to community groups to let them know what the body farm was all about. She hoped that having the facts straight from the experts would make people more open to the idea. According to the *Sydney Morning Herald*, this tactic worked: "After a presentation to Windsor Rotary [Club] in March, the club's newsletter reported that it was an 'extremely interesting (and at times a bit gruesomely illustrated) presentation.'"[24]

Emily Deschanel (third from the right) played forensic anthropologist Temperance Brennan on Bones. *The popularity of this show and others may help explain why body farms are gaining more acceptance.*

Within 4 months of when AFTER was officially announced, more than 30 people offered to donate their bodies when they died, and within a year, that number had risen to 500.

By the Numbers

16,000

approximate number of unsolved murders in Florida

A Growing Field

Because of tight budgets, unpopularity, and physical constraints, some body farms are necessarily small. For example, the Tennessee facility is set on a 2.5-acre (1 ha) wooded plot. The body farm at North Carolina's Western Carolina University is able to hold only about 10 bodies at a time, but the university also has a Human Identification Laboratory that is 1,100 square feet (102 sq m). This laboratory can hold more bodies as well as cremated remains. The Florida facility was proposed to be 5 acres (2 ha), but as of 2017, it is only 3.5 acres (1.4 ha); more money must be raised before the training facility can be built alongside the body farm.

However, as popularity has increased over the years and experts have seen the important contributions body farms make to the field of forensic science, some facilities have been able to gain more land. In Texas, Sam Houston State University's facility started at only 1 acre (0.4 ha), but as of 2017, it covers 247 acres (100 ha). Similarly, Texas State's facility started out at 5 acres (2 ha)—the largest in the world at that time—but eventually expanded to 26 acres (10.5 ha). The facility at Colorado Mesa University covers 35 acres (14 ha), and the one at the California University of Pennsylvania has 222 acres (89 ha). AFTER covers 119 acres (48 ha).

Although new facilities are private, experience has proven that they still need to be well protected. Before setting up the body farm in Knoxville, Bass worked cases for local law enforcement and stored murder victims' bodies in a vacant cow barn on land owned by the university. A prison was nearby, however, and inmates worked on the grounds near the barn. Bass soon noticed footprints inside, a sure sign that the corpses had attracted curious visitors. Sometimes the corpses were disarranged, too, proving that they were vulnerable to theft or vandalism. He remembered, "Nothing had been removed, but I didn't want to take the chance of losing a crucial piece of forensic evidence—a skull containing a telltale bullet, for instance."[25]

To keep vandals out, body farms generally surround their property with tall fences and other security measures.

Taking a lesson from Bass's difficulties, Western Carolina administrators do not publicize the exact location of their body farm to discourage curiosity seekers and intruders. They have also surrounded the facility with two fences, trees, and vegetation. AFTER learned from the experience of the United States body farms and is "situated well away from other properties, fully fenced with high-security screening and constantly monitored by CCTV [closed circuit television]."[26]

By the Numbers

3

number of hours it generally takes for rigor mortis to set in after death

---

Working Outside

Each body farm has its own way of doing things; there is no set of guidelines they all have to follow. However, there are some things each facility does because they are the best or most sensible ways. For instance, each facility generally places bodies inside a morgue refrigerator after they are donated. This keeps them from decaying before researchers are ready to study them. They are then marked with an identifier so their decomposition can be tracked over time, and when they are placed in the field, their location is mapped so they can easily be found again. The bodies are left alone to decay for a while so students can later practice finding and collecting the remains later.

There is no particular way body farms are required to identify their subjects. At the Knoxville site, each has a plastic tag strapped to an arm and an ankle and a sign nearby that states the same information. The tags identify its ethnicity, sex, age, and order of arrival. For instance, "WF 30 3/95" would indicate that a subject is a white female, 30 years old, and the third body to be placed in the outdoor lab in 1995. Other sites may have different codes.

Every time a researcher visits a body at any of the sites, the visit is carefully documented to maintain a chain of custody—chronological documentation showing who worked with the body, what was done or observed, and when. The chain of custody is an extremely important part of solving crimes because it proves that any clues found are accurate. If the chain of custody is not properly documented in a real case, a lawyer or judge may not allow the evidence to be submitted in court.

Because it is the purpose of outdoor

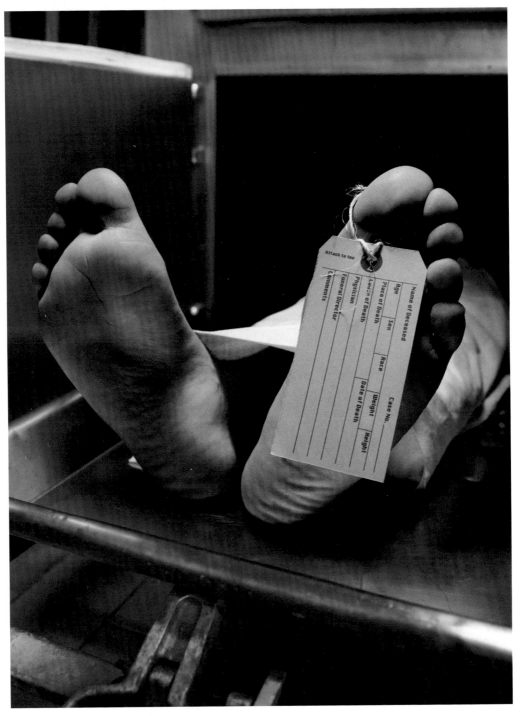

The tag reads:

Attach to toe

Name of Deceased | Case No.

Age | Sex | Race | Weight | Height

Place of Death

Cause of Death | Date of Death

Physician

Funeral Director

Comments

All corpses that come to the body farms are given identifying tags.

Flies lay eggs on dead bodies; the eggs then hatch into maggots (shown here), which help break down the body by eating the flesh.

Following the Chain of Custody

Chain of custody is the documented transfer of evidence from person to person from the moment the evidence is collected. This written record, arranged in order of date and time, lists who had control of the evidence and when. Police, crime scene investigators, and lab personnel follow chain-of-custody guidelines to ensure that evidence is not lost or tampered with and to prevent any misconduct—situations that can compromise a case in court. The guidelines are:

- Keep the number of people involved in collecting and handling evidence and documentation to a minimum.
- Only allow people associated with the case to handle the evidence and documentation.
- Always use proper chain-of-custody forms to document the transfer of evidence from person to person.
- Clearly and legibly identify evidence, fill out forms, and complete documentation using permanent ink.

labs to copy environmental conditions under which corpses decay, some bodies are positioned in open spaces where the sun is intense. Others are in shady areas. Some are on grass; some are buried under concrete. A few decay out of sight in hiding places that murderers often choose—an oil drum, a trash bin, or a car trunk. "What you'll see here is what's going to be happening at a real crime scene,"[27] said researcher Arpad Vass.

Bodies are in all stages of decomposition. The freshest look startlingly lifelike. Others are bloated and discolored, surrounded by flies and maggots, which are what fly eggs hatch into. Maggots eat the dead bodies, and an enzyme in their saliva breaks the bodies down so they decompose faster. Those that have been outdoors for several weeks are little more than brown skin and bones and tend to blend into the earth. In the autumn, rain and dead leaves cover them. In winter, depending on the climate, they are sometimes blanketed with snow. Many are left untouched until they are just skeletons, since forensic anthropologists only work with bones. Journalist Terry Moseley wrote of the Tennessee facility, "The farm is a morbid hybrid of serene woodland and violent crime scene. The silence is unsettling as you walk through ... land littered with exposed cadavers and body bags with an occasional decaying limb peeking out."[28]

Body farm researchers analyze tooth marks that raccoons and other scavengers leave on human bones so they can tell them apart from murder wounds.

The Smell of Decay

One of the first experiments Bass carried out at the Knoxville site was inspired by the discovery of a badly decayed corpse in a vacant lot on a busy Knoxville street in 1976. Neither neighbors nor passersby had noticed a smell of decay, and Bass wondered why. "If the human nose couldn't detect a body at that distance, at which distance could it detect a decomposing corpse? The answer would be useful not just to me ... but to police, firefighters, and search-and-rescue workers."[1]

To get an answer, Bass took one of his donated subjects that was bloated and foul smelling and hid it behind bushes and trees in a far corner of the body farm. He placed markers at 10-yard (9 m) intervals on the route leading to the corpse. He then led a group of students along the route, instructing them to tell him when they smelled something. The students did not react until they were between 10 and 20 yards (9 and 18 m) from the body. Bass noted, "The research was quick and dirty ... but it was good enough to show me that yes, you can die and decompose in a vacant lot ... and never be smelled by thousands of people passing by just fifty feet away."[2]

1. Bill Bass and Jon Jefferson, *Death's Acre: Inside the Legendary Forensic Lab the Body Farm Where the Dead Do Tell Tales*. New York, NY: Berkeley, 2003, e-book.

2. Bass and Jefferson, *Death's Acre*, e-book.

Identifying Animal and Insect Activity

Flies are everywhere at body farms, swarming in clouds over fresh bodies and researchers, looking for food and moist places to lay eggs. Bass and Jefferson wrote about the hardships endured by student Bill Rodriguez, who carried out some of the first insect studies in 1981: "Sitting just a foot or two away from a bloody body, Bill would soon find even himself overrun with flies, seeking ... any dark, damp orifices (including Bill's nostrils) to lay their eggs in. He quickly learned to wrap netting around his head to keep the flies out of his eyes, nose, mouth, and ears."[29] Flies leave once a body dries, but then there are other insects with which to cope. "I thought there would be a lot of flies and bugs, but all there was around was bees,"[30] said crime scene technician Dale Allison when he visited.

In addition to insects, larger predators visit. Crows and vultures may swoop down for a quick meal during the day, while raccoons and rats eat maggots and carry away small bones at night. Infrared cameras with motion detectors capture images of the night visitors, and researchers use their activities to learn to distinguish tooth or beak marks from injuries made by murderers. "We're always interested in separating human action from animal action,"[31] said Richard Jantz, former director of the Forensic Anthropology Center in Tennessee.

Studying the Bones

After the corpses are reduced to bones, they are transferred to indoor laboratories to be cleaned, examined, documented, and stored. Flies and the smell of decay are common in indoor labs, but overall, the spaces are much cleaner and more orderly than outdoors. There are a variety of kettles, saws, brushes, and tweezers for removing decayed flesh from bone. There are refrigerators and freezers to preserve remains, examining tables for studying them, and microscopes for analyzing tissue and bone at the cellular level. In these labs, workers piece broken bones together, take measurements, and prepare skeletons for storage.

Here they also carry out experiments that cannot be done outdoors, such as categorizing saw marks, making microscopic studies of bones that are burned or otherwise injured, and identifying unknown victims. As with the outdoor work, each body farm conducts different research, but the majority of research projects at all facilities focus on how to

Corpses are left outside at the body farm until they skeletonize, or are reduced to bones. Then, they are moved to the indoor lab to be cleaned and studied more closely.

determine age, sex, and PMI. The *Texas Tribune* described one research project being conducted in 2015 at the San Marcos site:

> One graduate student is working on a project that uses only teeth to determine the season of death. Each permanent tooth is anchored to gums twice a year [in a living person] by tiny, distinct fibers; a bright line is laid in the spring or summer and a dark line in the fall or winter. The number of bands, and the color and width of the outermost one, can help estimate the age at death and when a person died.[32]

Maintaining the chain of command is still a priority, and every step of each activity is carefully documented so the work will be seen as valid if it is used in criminal cases later.

Signing Up for the Body Farm

In order for work to be carried out on body farms, researchers need a continuous supply of corpses. In 1981, the year Bass opened his facility, only four became available. In following years, numbers increased, and some subjects were homeless men and women who had no family to claim them when they died. Others were unidentified crime victims, such as a woman who was found floating in the Tennessee River or a man who appeared to be a victim of a drug deal gone wrong. By 2000, however, most subjects were people whose bodies had been donated by family members. As the knowledge and popularity of body farms grows, many people also sign up to have their bodies donated after they die. The North Carolina site, which can only hold a maximum of 10 bodies at a time, had to put a hold on accepting donations from July 1, 2017, through September 4, 2017. When the Florida site was announced, about 30 people signed up to donate their bodies when they die. In the meantime, the Florida body farm started with four donated bodies. Its official name—the Adam Kennedy Memorial Forensics Field—came from the first donation.

Some people have raised questions about the ethics of using bodies donated by family members rather than by people who have signed up to donate their own body. Caitlin Doughty, a former funeral home employee, started an organization called The Order of the Good Death to help change the way Western society currently views death. When asked about her views on body farms, she said,

> I hadn't realized that 60 percent of donations were made by families not pre-registered. Being laid

out to be decomposed in the elements and poked and prodded and studied seems like something you should really be comfortable with before [death]. It's that same problem that I had with my mortuary school practicing embalming on indigent [homeless] bodies from the county morgue. Not inherently wrong (as there is no wrong way to handle a dead body), just

something I suspect they wouldn't want us doing if they had a choice in life to say no.[33]

Roy Crawford, a mining engineer from Kentucky, decided to donate his body for several reasons. "I like the idea that one day research done on my body might be used to catch a murderer," he said. "I [also] look at the [body farm] as a scientific laboratory in nature, and

Bodies are placed in many different situations at body farms, including inside car trunks.

I think nature is beautiful. The idea of being propped up against a tree to decompose sounds a whole lot better than being locked in a box and preserved under the ground."[34]

There is no cost to donate, although those who live some distance away are responsible for arranging and paying for transportation to the facility. All facilities provide donation forms online that can be filled out and submitted. Medical histories are requested so researchers can look for and document the physical effects of cancer, heart disease, injuries, and the like. A photograph is requested as well so forensic artists who reconstruct facial features from skulls can sharpen their skills. Individuals who have contracted HIV/AIDS, hepatitis, tuberculosis, or antibiotic-resistant bacterial infections are not accepted due to the danger of infecting researchers.

Those who donate their bodies often imagine themselves decaying in a peaceful spot, such as under a shady tree. However, no one can say where their body will be placed, or of what project they will be a part. They can be sure, however, that no matter where their remains are situated, they will be treated with as much respect as any living person. Murray Marks, a pathology professor at the University of Tennessee, said, "I cannot divorce myself from the fact that I am the caretaker of these people. I respect this incredibly precious gift."[35]

Chapter Three
Making Important Discoveries

The first body farm was created so researchers could find the answers to simple questions. Researcher Rebecca Wilson said those questions included, "How do we decompose? What do we look like at different stages of decomposition? If I have a body that's been dead for three days, what does that look like and can I tell you it's been dead for three days?"[36]

The research done at body farms helps answer those questions, and as more becomes known about the decomposition process, researchers have moved on to more complex questions, often using the latest technology to help them in their task. For instance, around 2013, the San Marcos facility began flying drones over the body farm and photographing the ground below. In the black and white photographs, the "gray landscape was grass and dirt and the white spots denoted excessive vegetation. The black flecks were decomposing corpses."[37] This experiment proved that if a plane equipped with a powerful camera took pictures of the ground, researchers who knew what to look for would be able to study the pictures and find dead bodies that might not be immediately apparent.

Learning About Decomposition

The first step in learning about human decomposition involved observing the corpse as it decayed. The task was simple but time-consuming. From the moment a subject was placed in the outdoor lab, someone was assigned to watch it, photograph it, and record every detail of the changes that occurred. Observation had to take place almost nonstop in the beginning because decomposition progresses very quickly. Researchers did not want to miss a single detail that might be significant. Later, the corpse was visited every day or two because changes occurred more slowly.

Students who had never seen a decaying body before were often repulsed and sickened when they began the observation process. They soon adjusted, however, to disturbing sights such as wasps crawling in and out of a subject's mouth or crows tearing at a subject's intestines. They also came to accept death and decay as ugly but natural processes from which much could be learned. Forensic anthropologist and former body farm student Emily Craig remembered, "Somehow, the shocking had become commonplace, and the human remains I saw rotting in the sun had begun to look more like three-dimensional puzzles and less like once-living human beings."[38] Soon, instead of gagging and vomiting, the students were able to watch the movement of thousands of maggots as they disarrayed clothing, making it seem like the corpse had been searched when it actually had not been. They noted that decompositional fluids seeped from the body, destroying all vegetation under the corpse and staining the ground black.

They saw large predators scatter and carry away bones, leaving confusing results for law enforcement officials to decipher.

The most significant observations were of the decay process itself. Under all but the most extreme conditions, it occurred in a predictable progression, the first stage of which Bass called the "fresh" phase. This begins about four minutes after death and ends when the body becomes visibly bloated. During the fresh phase, the corpse resembles an unconscious, living person. Despite being fresh, however, it attracts flies, which lay eggs in wounds and body openings. The eggs hatch into thousands of maggots, which begin eating the flesh. At the same time, bacteria in the intestines invade other parts of the body and start breaking down tissues.

By the Numbers

500

number of eggs a female housefly can lay in its 28-day lifetime

Pigs Are Not Good Enough

Pigs and humans are similar enough that pig organs can be transplanted into humans, so for many years, researchers studied the rate at which pigs decomposed and applied those results to human corpses. However, recent research by the Knoxville body farm shows that pigs and humans decompose differently, which means time of death determined by using pigs may no longer be admissible evidence in court. The research team left five pigs, five rabbits, and five humans outside in winter, spring, and summer to compare their decomposition rates. According to *Science Alert*,

> In the end, they found that all of the test subjects decomposed [at] vastly different rates—with pigs decomposing faster than humans on average—and that the human body varied more wildly from body to body than the rabbits or pigs did. Specific body decay times weren't released, but the information [led] the researchers to conclude that pigs—or any other animals—cannot be used to accurately predict a time of death in a human.[1]

These results show how important body farms are to the field of forensic science.

1. Josh Hrala, "Human 'Body Farm' Reveals We Need to Stop Using Pigs to Establish Time of Death," *Science Alert*, June 17, 2016. www.sciencealert.com/pigs-may-not-be-the-most-amazing-forensic-tool-after-all-finds-body-farm-researchers.

Bloating

As bacteria attack the body, gases such as methane, hydrogen sulfide, putrescine, and cadaverine are produced inside the corpse, and it enters the second, or "bloat," phase. The body swells up, and the skin takes on a reddish-brown color. Fatty tissues break down under the skin and give it a glossy shine. Arteries, veins, and capillaries become visible as purplish-red lines, similar to rivers on a map. Eventually, the skin splits and falls off in large sheets. Maggots eat away large portions of flesh, creating gaping holes.

The "decay" stage follows bloating. At this point, the combination of maggot and bacterial activity finally breaks down skin and flesh enough so the body deflates, leaving the belly shrunken and the rib cage jutting upward. Tissue grows soft, decomposition fluids ooze into the soil, and the gut-wrenching smell of decay becomes extremely strong. M. Lee Goff, a former forensic entomologist and professor, observed, "I have noted a strong correlation between the onset of the Decay Stage and a rise in absences and sick days

In the second stage of decomposition, the body produces gases that cause it to bloat, or swell. A bloated body such as the one shown here will float on water, while a newly dead or skeletonized body will sink.

among my graduate students."[39] By the end of the decay stage, 80 percent of the corpse's body weight has decomposed, leaving mostly skin and bone behind.

Bass calls the final stage of decomposition the "dry" stage, although some experts consider this same period to be two stages: post-decay and skeletal. During post-decay, remains are dry and any remaining skin and hair on the skeleton is slowly eaten by insects. During the skeletal stage, the bones break down. Heat, water, and acids in the soil cause organic material to leach away, and delicate minerals that remain eventually crumble to dust.

Tracking Decomposition

At the same time that Bass and his students became familiar with every observable change produced by decomposition, they timed the changes. In Tennessee, a body was fresh for no more than 3 days; bloating could last from day 4 to day 10; the decay stage generally lasted to day 20; and post-decay lasted up until about day 50. The skeletal phase was the longest and could continue up to a year or more, although at body farms, researchers generally end this phase within several months. "Normally we don't leave a body out there longer than a year because then the sun begins to bleach [the bones] and they'll crack,"[40] explained Bass. This would make it difficult for forensic anthropologists to study them.

Bass knew that his decomposition timeline was variable, however. Experience had taught him that climate, environment, and insect activity

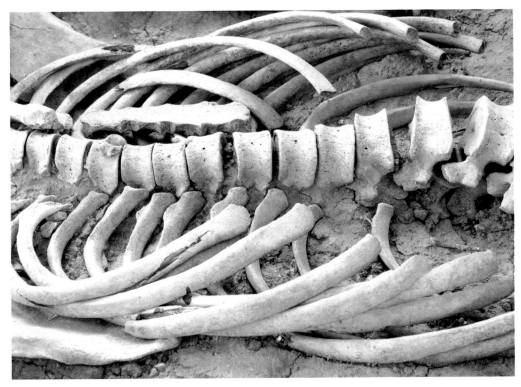

Climate is one factor that changes the appearance of flesh and bones.

interacted to speed or slow the process. Bodies found in hot, dry locations such as Nevada, for instance, dry so fast that the bloat and decay stages are virtually absent. The result is not a skeleton, but a mummified body with flesh and skin intact. In contrast, bodies found on a Kansas prairie rapidly decay to clean bones. "Kansas corpses tended to be clean, sun-bleached skeletons, like something you'd see in a Hollywood western,"[41] Bass and Jefferson explained.

Before establishing the body farm, Bass and other forensic experts had only guessed at factors that caused differences in decay. They presumed that bodies were more likely to become maggot infested in Tennessee, for instance, because humidity and vegetation produced large insect populations. However, they did not know for sure if this was true, so they set out to learn exactly how insect activity, climate, and environment worked together so variations could be explained. When body farms were established in other parts of the country as well as Australia, researchers in those facilities began to do the same for their parts of the world, too.

The Role of Insects

The field of forensic entomology—the study of insects as they relate to crime—was badly overlooked by

By the Numbers

600

number of species of insects that can visit a body from death through the skeletal stage

experts over the years. In fact, prior to the 1990s, if law enforcement officials found maggots on a body at a crime scene, they washed them away before conducting an autopsy. Few dreamed that maggots could tell them how long the body had been lying where it was found.

As one of their first projects, body farm researchers began watching the coming and going of insects throughout the decay process. It soon became clear that there was a pattern of arrival of insects, which is called faunal (animal) succession. The pattern of succession was predictable, although there were variations in species depending on location and time of year. Flies were the most reliable, always arriving within minutes of death and before other insects. They could also be counted on to quickly lay thousands of eggs that resembled piles of sawdust on the corpse.

Shortly after flies deposited their eggs,

Forensic entomologists study the hundreds of varieties of bugs that visit corpses.

Occupation: Forensic Entomologist

Job Description:
A forensic entomologist studies insects found at crime scenes in order to determine the PMI, whether the body has been moved, and how the victim died. Work takes place both in the laboratory and in the field. In addition to helping law enforcement officials, forensic entomologists often teach and perform research at a college or university, act as consultants, and provide continuing education classes to law enforcement officials.

Education:
Aspiring forensic entomologists must earn a bachelor of science (BS) degree in entomology or a related field such as biology, plus a master of science (MS) degree that includes coursework in forensics and entomology. Most forensic entomologists also earn a doctor of philosophy (PhD) degree in entomology and become certified by the American Board of Forensic Entomology.

Qualifications:
Aspiring forensic entomologists must be objective, be determined, and enjoy working with insects. They must be able to handle situations involving death and decay.

Salary:
$56,000 to $85,000 per year

a variety of beetles arrived. Some, such as rove beetles, hister beetles, and carrion beetles, invaded the corpse to feast on eggs and maggots. As the corpse dried, however, they moved away, and ham beetles and hide beetles arrived to feed on the skin, exposed tendons, and bones. When nothing but bones were left, most of the insects left, too, but researchers found that tiny herbivorous soil beetles and springtails (six-legged, wingless insects) that had migrated to the soil under the corpse persisted for an indefinite period of time.

Interpreting the Results

With new opportunities to study insects and human decomposition, numerous entomologists came to the body farm in Tennessee to carry out studies over the years. Their research projects were designed to be practical, and the results were quickly applied to crime solving. For instance, they were able to tell law enforcement that when organisms such as springtails and mites were found in soil, a body had once been at that location, even if it was no longer there. If a body showed unexpected areas of maggot infestation and advanced decomposition, they could assume that the victim had sustained wounds in those areas because flies are drawn to blood. If blood-sucking insects such as lice were found on a victim, that insect could be analyzed to see if it contained the murderer's DNA (deoxyribonucleic acid, which is genetic material unique to each human being) and perhaps identify them.

The most significant research produced the breakthrough discovery that insects could be used to help determine the PMI. Calculations were generally based on fly life cycles: The flies arrive and lay eggs on a body, the eggs hatch, and larvae grow and shed their hard exoskeletons according to very predictable timetables. For instance, at a temperature of 80.6 degrees Fahrenheit (27 degrees Celsius), *Calliphora vicina* (bluebottle blowfly) eggs hatch 24 hours after being laid. First generation (instar) maggots eat and grow for 24 hours. They then molt (shed their skin) and enter the second instar stage, which lasts 20 hours. Another molt puts them in the third instar stage, which lasts 48 hours, after which they go into the prepupa stage. Within the next 128 hours, they stop eating, move away from the body, form a hard protective shell known as a puparium, and go into a resting stage. That final stage lasts for 11 days, after which they hatch as adults.

The process of determining the PMI using flies first required identifying the species and age of the maggots on a body when it was found. Researchers then calculated backward to see when the eggs were laid. For instance, if bluebottle blowfly maggots on a body were second instar size, crime scene investigators could know with certainty that they had been deposited on the body three days earlier, so that was likely when death had occurred.

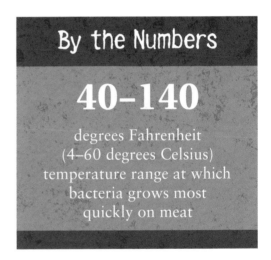

By the Numbers

40–140

degrees Fahrenheit (4–60 degrees Celsius) temperature range at which bacteria grows most quickly on meat

The Role of Weather

Temperature also has to be taken into consideration because of its effect on decomposition. Meat, including human tissue, spoils more quickly in warm temperatures than in cold, and there are more insects active on warm days than on cold ones. The exact correlation between temperature and decay was unknown, however, so researchers set out to learn more about it. For instance, they placed one body in the sun and a comparable one in the shade, and they documented the differences in speed at which they broke down. They also noted previously uncharted variables, such as the fact that in sunny locations both the body and the ground absorbed and held heat. That warmth allowed bacteria and larvae activity to continue into the night when cooler air temperatures ought to have slowed activity down.

Other temperature-related factors such as seasons and climate had to be considered, too. Long summer days produced conditions favorable to bacteria and insects and speeded up decomposition. When days shortened, decay slowed because of shorter periods of warmth. Cold-weather climates acted like freezers in the winter, preserving a body and extending the decomposition period for months longer than expected.

Humidity was another important climate variable. When combined with warm temperatures, humidity increased the speed of decomposition dramatically. On humid summer days in Tennessee, for instance, bodies were found to completely decompose in as little as 18 days.

Researchers have found that the colder the weather, the more slowly a body decomposes.

What Factors Affect Decay?

In a human body, the rate and manner of decomposition is affected by a number of factors. From greatest to least effect, they include:

- temperature
- availability of oxygen
- embalming
- cause of death
- whether the body was buried and how deep it was buried
- access by scavengers
- trauma, including wounds and crushing blows
- humidity or wetness
- rainfall
- body size and weight
- presence or absence of clothing
- the surface on which the body rests

On the other hand, too much moisture, such as when a body was placed in water, slowed decomposition because tissues did not dry enough to attract insects that normally colonized the body during the late decay stages.

Using Math to Determine PMI

Because temperature had such a significant impact on insect activity and decomposition, researchers found a way to mathematically factor it into their calculations when determining PMI. They developed the concept of accumulated degree hours (ADH) and accumulated degree days (ADD). Using these variables, insect development and decomposition rates could be standardized by multiplying the amount of time and the temperature. For example, Bass and Jefferson explained, "Ten consecutive 70-degree days in summertime would total 700 ADDs [10 x 70]; so would 20 wintertime days averaging 35 degrees apiece [20 x 35]. In either season, winter or summer, a body at 700 accumulated degree days would exhibit similar signs of decomposition."[42] To calculate ADH, researchers turned to tables published by entomologists in the 1950s that give the developmental times for various fly species at controlled laboratory temperatures. They could multiply the developmental time and the temperature to get the answer they needed.

Determining the PMI based on insect activity and using ADH or ADD was somewhat complicated but effective. Researchers took maggots collected from a body and raised them to adults in a laboratory at a constant temperature. When they hatched, the ADH for the time they had been in the lab was noted, their species was identified from their appearance, and the total ADH for that species under laboratory conditions was determined from tables. The ADH for the time in the lab was deducted from the total ADH; the remainder was the ADH the maggots were on the body before it was discovered. That remainder was divided by the average crime scene temperature to find the number of hours the maggots were developing on the body at the crime scene. Counting back that number of hours from the time the body was discovered gave the approximate time death occurred.

Studying the Variables

As researchers grew to better understand the way insects, temperature, and climate combined to affect decomposition, they realized unique conditions in the environment immediately around the corpse could affect the process, too. For instance, a corpse lying in the desert might be expected to dehydrate and mummify at a certain rate, but if that corpse happened to be resting in the shade of a boulder in that desert, it would be in a slightly cooler environment and would

Bodies wrapped in cloth or plastic decompose more slowly than uncovered bodies.

perhaps dehydrate more slowly. A body lying in an airy, open living room of a house would quickly attract flies, but if it was shut in a closet in that living room, it would not.

To learn exactly how important a role the environment played, more studies were conducted, mimicking real-life victims and the types of conditions under which they died. Bass recalled, "[We] compared bodies on land to bodies submerged in water; the floaters lasted twice as long. [We] compared bodies on the surface to bodies buried in graves, ranging from shallow to deep; the deeply buried bodies took eight times as long to decompose as the exposed bodies."[43] Researchers compared overweight corpses to thin ones; surprisingly, the overweight ones skeletonized faster because their flesh fed a larger number of maggots. Corpses that were hanged decayed less quickly than ones on the ground because maggots fell off the body and were not able to get back on to consume it. Burned corpses decayed faster than unburned ones because small cracks in the skin allowed insects to penetrate the flesh more easily.

Bodies were studied clothed and naked; those that were naked generally decomposed faster because insects could get to body openings faster. Researchers had to add at least two days to their estimates for decomposition if a body was wrapped in a tarp because flies could not access it as quickly as if it were uncovered.

Using the Bones

No matter how many studies were conducted, there were always new questions that needed to be answered. Many of the questions involved bones. Bass himself had always been particularly fascinated by bones. They were his specialty, and he knew they could provide much information about how a person died. For this reason, after corpses skeletonize at a body farm, the bones are collected and transferred to a laboratory for analysis.

Chapter Four
Down to the Bone

Looking at bones is the most important part of a forensic anthropologist's job. To a trained expert, bones give an enormous amount of information about a person. Through experiments carried out over the years in labs around the world—especially at body farms—researchers now know how to use a skeleton to determine many things. They can generally tell the sex, race, and age of a victim from their bones, but they can also sometimes tell the time, place, and manner of a person's death. For instance, if a skeleton's ribs have notch marks on them, that may indicate the person was stabbed. The more bodies they study, the more experts learn.

Preparing the Bones

Staff and students have to be thoroughly familiar with bones before carrying out research. They learn early on that the adult human skeleton contains 206 bones, which are divided into 4 classes—long, short, flat, and irregular. They become so familiar with each that they can identify even a small piece of bone without difficulty. They know exactly how a skeleton falls apart as it decays and the ligaments, tendons, cartilage, and muscles disappear. Emily Craig wrote, "When a corpse is laid out on the ground, gravity sucks the bones downward so that the skeleton eventually collapses, settling into earth made soft and soggy from the decaying tissues. What once was a rib cage becomes a flat row of rib bones, while the spine turns into a collection of disarticulated [disconnected] vertebrae."[44]

It is the task of graduate students at body farms to collect a subject's bones after a decomposition project is complete. Putting on gloves and glasses to protect themselves from disease-causing bacteria, they pick up each piece, check its name off a list, and carefully place it in a collection bag. Trowels and a metal screen are used at the end of collection so even tiny finger and toe bones hidden in dirt and debris can be recovered.

Once the bones are retrieved, they are taken to the indoor lab where the cleaning process begins. Again wearing safety glasses and gloves, researchers put the bones in large stainless steel kettles that are filled with water, detergent, and bleach. "Sometimes we have to cut them apart to fit,"[45] said Texas State anthropology professor Michelle Hamilton, who was a graduate assistant at the University of Tennessee before becoming a professor at Texas State University.

Electric slow cookers are set up to hold smaller bones such as skulls, hands, and feet. Everything is simmered on low heat, filling the air with the smell of decay

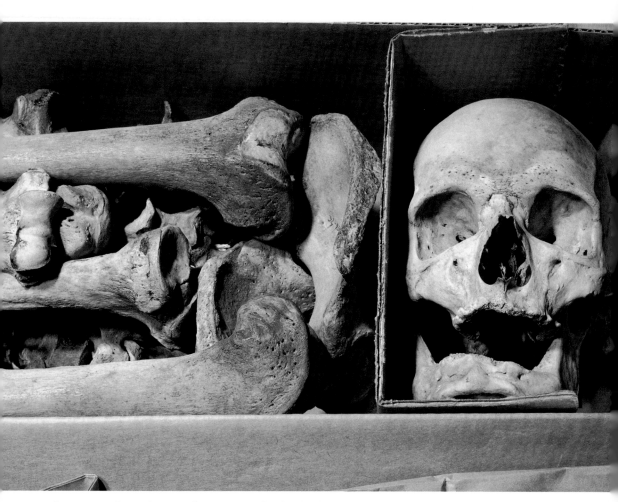

After researchers clean and examine a body, the bones are stored in a specially designed box such as this one.

TV Myths versus Reality

TV shows involving forensic scientists have become incredibly popular in the past two decades. However, the job is often misrepresented on the shows to make it more exciting to watch. Some myths spread by TV shows include:

- *Forensic scientists only solve murders*: There are many reasons why a body may need to be identified, and most of them involve accidental death—for instance, if a person had a heart attack while jogging alone. Murders are much rarer than TV shows make them seem.
- *Forensic science is thrilling*: TV shows try to be exciting so they can attract viewers, and they generally try to keep the cast of characters small so viewers can keep track of them all. This means they often show forensic scientists arresting and questioning suspects, and sometimes getting into dangerous situations. In reality, the majority of a forensic scientist's work is done in the lab; sometimes they will go out into the field to collect evidence, but other times it will be brought to them. Additionally, real-life lab work is generally not interesting to watch, so TV shows often do not show forensic scientists laying out the bones of a body piece by piece or comparing bones from multiple bodies.
- *Tests are completed and crimes are solved quickly*: Tests for DNA and the presence of any poisons that might be in the body seem to be completed within minutes or hours on TV, but in reality, they take weeks. This means a crime may not be solved for months or even years. TV shows often speed up the process so the show can be wrapped up within an hour.
- *Evidence is foolproof*: On TV, it seems as if forensic scientists can figure out a murder case with 100 percent certainty. In reality, evidence can often be interpreted several different ways, and forensic scientists must use their skills to make their best guess about what happened. According to the website Criminal Justice Degrees Guide, "This idea, known as the 'CSI Effect,' is actually affecting real-life trials. Juries expect to be given a show and hard evidence like they've seen on TV, and when they don't get it, they often don't think the case is strong enough."[1]

1. "10 Forensic Myths Spread by TV," Criminal Justice Degrees Guide, accessed July 31, 2017. www.criminaljusticedegreesguide.com/features/10-forensic-myths-spread-by-tv.html.

and cooked meat, until most of the flesh falls off. The bones are then removed from the pots; cleaned with scissors, tweezers, and toothbrushes; and laid out to dry. After examination, they are coated with a preservative and placed in specially designed boxes. The boxes are labeled with the age, sex, and race of the subject, and then shelved on tall metal racks in storage rooms. Journalist Terry Moseley wrote, "Regardless of the size of the adult body in life, almost every skeleton can be neatly tucked into a box measuring 3 feet by 1 foot by 1 foot."[46]

Looking for Clues

Examination of the bones after they are cleaned gives researchers important information needed to solve cases. Identity can be determined by matching teeth found in a skull to a missing person's dental records. If no dental records are available, teeth can still be useful to determine the age of the victim so police can narrow their search. If the victim only has baby teeth, for instance, investigators know they are looking for a child younger than five years old. If all permanent teeth are present, the victim is at least 17 years old. Worn or missing teeth may indicate an older victim.

The state of other bones can also help determine an unidentified victim's age. Microscopic examination of thin slices of long bones can reveal the condition of osteons—structural units—which fragment as a person ages. The disappearance of cartilage at the end of long bones and between other bones is another sign of maturity. Porous, ragged, and sharp edges on ribs and pelvic bones are sure signs of approaching old age.

The sex of the victim can also be determined from the bones. Male bones are normally larger than female bones, and bony knobs where muscles attach are heavier on males because men have larger muscles than women. Male skulls are easy to identify because of their heavy brow ridges, and they have a large knob called the external occipital condyle at the base of their skull where several neck muscles attach. On the other hand, the female pelvic inlet (the space in the middle of the pelvic bone) is larger than a male's because a baby must be able to pass through during the birthing process.

Bones can also indicate ethnicity. In general, skull bones of individuals of African descent, which anthropologists call Negroid, are heavier and smoother than those of Asians (Mongoloid), Native Americans, and Caucasians (Caucasoid). Negroid eye sockets tend to be more wide-set, and their nasal openings tend to be broader. Caucasoid skulls are noticeably long and thin, while Mongoloid skulls are rounder than other racial groups. In Mongoloid skulls as well, eye sockets are round, cheekbones are flat, and front teeth show ridging on the inside edges that can be distinctive.

Noticing these traits can help police identify a body, but they are not

male female

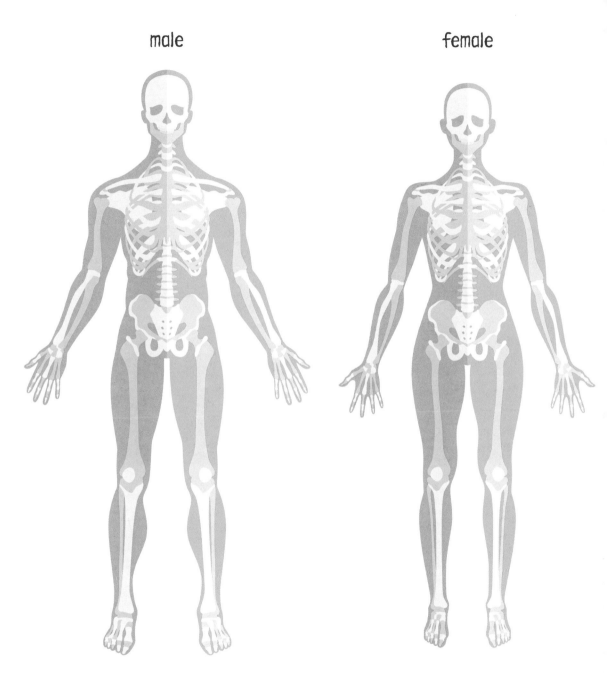

Over the years, researchers have learned how to identify differences between male and female skeletons.

Facial reconstruction sculptors use markers to help them note a person's tissue depth.

Examining the Evidence

Whenever a badly decayed corpse is found, crime scene investigators do their best to create a biological profile to help identify the victim. In her book, *Teasing Secrets from the Dead*, forensic anthropologist Emily Craig explained how bones and other evidence are important aids in creating that profile:

Every biological profile ... would ideally include the anthropologist's "Big Four": sex, age, race, and stature. If you're lucky, and you've got the evidence to go further, you can put in ancillary [secondary] information such as weight and maybe hair color. Often, human remains do survive with enough intact hair to determine color, because hair is made up of dead cells, which don't decompose as soft tissues do. Even a single long, blond hair found stuck to the underside of a skull can help tremendously when you are trying to identify skeletal remains.

Sometimes the associated evidence—evidence found with a body or remains—can give you a clue. Clothing, for example, can help you determine a person's weight and size, though, of course, it too tends to decompose. In the end, though, the bones last longest—and they hold many secrets if you know what to look for.[1]

1. Emily Craig, *Teasing Secrets from the Dead: My Investigations at America's Most Infamous Crime Scenes.* New York, NY: Crown, 2004, p. 55.

foolproof. For instance, a particular gene commonly found in Asians or Native Americans causes something known as "tooth shoveling," where the upper teeth are scoop-shaped rather than flat. This trait is almost never found in people of African or European descent. However, a person who looks European may have tooth shoveling if they have Asian or Native American ancestors. This is why facial reconstruction is an important tool.

Facial reconstruction is done by a sculptor who is trained in facial anatomy. The sculptor generally makes a plaster cast of a skull, then uses plastic markers to note how many layers of clay should be applied to each part of the face. Using this method, a sculptor can give law enforcement and forensic experts an idea of what a person looked like when they have only the skull to work with.

Always Learning

Because bones are constantly being studied, new information and new means of identifying unknown victims are discovered regularly. For instance, in the early 1990s, Craig entered Bass's PhD program and attended his human identification class. As usual, during the first semester, Bass asked the class to identify the ethnicity of a skeleton. The request was a trick. The bones had come from a black man, but the skull had no Negroid characteristics. No one had ever identified the skeleton correctly. Even Bass had mistakenly identified it as Caucasoid until X-rays of a known missing person proved him wrong.

Bass expected everyone in the class to misidentify the skeleton, so he was surprised when Craig correctly stated that the victim had been black. Thinking that she had cheated and gotten the information from a former student, Bass confronted her: "How did you know? *Everybody* gets that wrong. They take one look at that skull and they're sure it's Caucasoid."[47]

Craig explained that she had not based her answer on the shape of the skull. She had looked at the knee. During the course of her former career as a medical illustrator, she had looked at thousands of knee joints, and she had observed that the angle of the intercondylar notch (a small groove at the end of the thigh bone) was different in Caucasoid skeletons than in Negroid ones. Bass was fascinated and encouraged Craig to do further research on knees. As a result, she invented a formula that allows law enforcement to differentiate Negroid and Caucasoid femurs with 90 percent accuracy.

Bones and Violence

In addition to finding new ways to identify unknown victims, body farm researchers study bones to better translate acts of violence into evidence. First, they note the variations in shape and thickness that result from bones being broken and healed. They learn to recognize the difference between bones that were injured when the victim was alive, those that were injured at the time of death, and those that were injured long after death. Craig wrote, "The nature of bone changes ... radically after the body dies. When a person is alive or very recently dead, his or her bones resemble green wood. If you stick a knife into what we call a 'green bone,' you can pry up a little sliver, because the bone—living tissue—is still pliable. If you try to make the same cut days or weeks after death, the bone is more like firewood—dead and dried-out wood."[48]

Researchers not only learn to recognize signs of past abuse in bones that have been injured and then healed, they

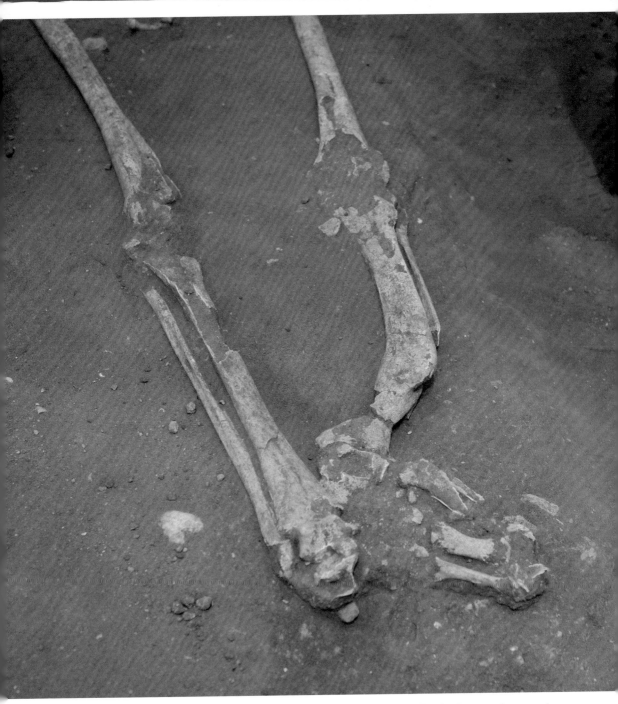

It is important for forensic anthropologists to be able to tell whether marks on a bone, such as the one above this skeleton's left ankle, are the result of an old or new injury.

can also identify the crushing caused by hammers and tire irons, as well as the nicks, punctures, and slices caused by sharp objects such as knives, axes, and scissors. They recognize the pattern of fractures that are a result of a body being struck or run over by a car. They know bullet holes in skulls leave distinctive entry and exit marks and that bullets striking bones can chip or shatter them, depending on the angle of impact. Researcher Corey Sparks made a special study of the trajectory (curved path) of bullets as they entered and left a skull using digital scans and a computer. In the course of his project, he worked on a murder case in which a man claimed to have accidentally killed his wife while cleaning his rifle. Sparks explained, "We scanned her skull … and we found that the bullet had to have come from directly above her. So we proved it was murder."[49]

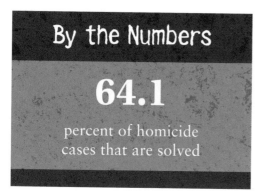

By the Numbers

64.1

percent of homicide cases that are solved

Preserving the Bones

No matter what the bones look like, body farm administrators are careful to preserve them for future generations to study. Over the years, the Forensic Anthropology Center in Tennessee has come to house the world's largest collection of modern skeletons. The collection includes the William M. Bass Forensic Skeletal Collection, which consists of more than 100 complete and partial skeletons, most of them unidentified. There is also the WM Bass Donated Skeletal Collection, which contains complete skeletons of more than 1,800 identified individuals. Each has been carefully measured as well as scanned using computerized axial tomography, creating three-dimensional images. The collection is unique because of the diversity of its subjects. Early collections generally contained only older Caucasians, but the Bass collection includes Caucasians, Africans, and Latinx with birth years ranging from 1892 to 2016. The collection is also unique because it illustrates how bones change as a result of societal changes, such as better eating habits, less hard labor, and improved medical care. Former director Richard Jantz pointed out, "We're taller than we were more than 100 years ago. The shape of the skull is higher, narrower, and longer. The teeth and jaws, like the rest of the skeleton, are experiencing less stress, so they are becoming smaller."[50]

What Happens in a Fire?

While studying burned bodies, body farm researchers found that fire caused muscles to contract in predictable ways, leaving clear evidence for investigators to find. According to Bill Bass,

The arms and legs are the first to go. Relatively thin and surrounded by oxygen, they're like kindling, easy to ignite and quick to burn. At temperatures of only a few hundred degrees ... the flesh begins to burn. As it does, something remarkable and eerie happens. The limbs begin to move—the hands and feet clench, the arms curl up toward the shoulders, and the legs spread slightly apart with the knees flexed ... The flexors, the muscles that cause our arms and legs to bend, are stronger than the extensors, the ones that cause our limbs to straighten. As fire cooks and dries out the muscles and tendons of the body, they shrink, just like steak on the grill, and the flexors overpower the extensors.

The resulting position is very much like a boxer's stance in the ring; for that reason we call it the "pugilistic posture" ... If ... the arms are tied or pinned behind the back, they won't be able to curl up, so finding a burned body whose arms are straight can be an important clue that the victim was somehow confined or restrained.[1]

1. Bill Bass and Jon Jefferson, *Death's Acre: Inside the Legendary Forensic Lab the Body Farm Where the Dead Do Tell Tales*. New York, NY: Berkeley, 2003, e-book.

As technology improved over the years, Jantz organized what had been learned about the skeletal collections into a forensic data bank. The data bank contains detailed skeletal information from individuals worldwide and helps forensic scientists more easily determine the race and ethnicity of unknown remains. Dozens of groups, from Europeans to Australian Aborigines, are included in the files.

Using data-bank information in the 1990s, Jantz and computer expert Stephen Ousley created software named FORDISC (forensic discriminant function analysis), designed to aid others in identifying skeletal remains. FORDISC is based on measurements of thousands of bones and is continually being updated with data from body farm researchers and other forensic anthropologists. When a set of remains needs to be identified, bone measurements are entered into the computer, the numbers

By the Numbers

40,000

number of unidentified
bodies in American
evidence rooms

are compared with the database, and a classification of racial or ethnic origin is given. The program is used by international tribunals investigating war crimes, in human rights investigations, and by law enforcement seeking to identify a victim. In one 1991 case, for instance, police had unsuccessfully searched records of missing Caucasian males in order to identify a set of remains. After measurements of the remains were entered into FORDISC, it indicated that the victim was black, and he was then quickly identified. Bass and Jefferson wrote, "In several ... US murder cases ... [FORDISC] has played a pivotal role in focusing or refocusing efforts to identify unknown victims."[51]

Chapter Five
Technological Advancements

In the past, researchers relied on their observations alone to learn about bodies. Comparing multiple bodies allowed experts to learn the differences and similarities between skeletons, and the field of forensic science has made incredible accomplishments in the years since the first body farm was created. However, as technology has advanced, it has helped experts make even greater strides. Using chemical analysis, drones, infrared technology, and more, researchers are able to gain a deeper understanding of exactly what happens in a decomposing body and how to decode the secrets it holds. "Hi-tech is where it's going," said Richard Jantz in 2007. "I can see us doing a lot more biochemical work. I can see us doing more DNA work and DNA degradation."[52]

Examining the Dirt

One researcher who focuses on decay at the molecular level is Arpad A. Vass, who began working at the Knoxville body farm in the late 1980s and has since taken a position in the Life Sciences Division of Oak Ridge National Laboratory (ORNL), about 25 miles (40 km) from Knoxville. He remains a regular visitor to the body farm, as well as an assistant professor of forensic anthropology at the University of Tennessee.

Vass initially believed he could come up with a new method of determining time of death through bacterial analysis. He hoped to prove that bacteria developed on a dead body in succession patterns similar to those of insects. When he attempted to carry out his experiments, however, he realized the idea was impractical. The corpse he laid out was immediately flooded by so many species of bacteria that it was impossible to keep track of them. He wrote, "I came to the conclusion ... that with the exception of micro-organisms living in deep sea vents, every micro-organism known is involved in some aspect of the human decompositional cycle."[53] Technology has improved to the point that it is easier for researchers to study changes in the necrobiomes, or bacterial communities, on corpses. On December 22, 2016, researchers at the Knoxville site published a paper describing their work in this area:

In the study, the researchers took samples of bacteria from the ear and nasal canals of the cadavers and put them outdoors, leaving them to decompose naturally over the course of several weeks. They then sequenced the DNA of the bacteria, and used their findings to construct a model that could predict a body's time of death up to 55 "accumulated degree days."[54]

However, in the 1980s, DNA sequencing was not as advanced, so it was more difficult to study bacteria at the time. Abandoning his bacterial focus, Vass looked for another possible means of determining time since death. No one had studied the fluids that ooze out of a corpse, so he began researching those, taking samples of soil from under the body and doing a molecular analysis of the decay byproducts found in it. He discovered that those byproducts contain a mixture of fatty acids—carbon-based molecules found throughout the body—released when organs and tissues decay.

Studying them, Vass noted that the ratio of the fatty acids to one another changed as the body decomposed.

Using seven subjects—two black males, a white female, and four white males—who were laid out in the body farm at various times of the year, Vass collected his soil byproduct data every three days in the spring and summer, and weekly in the fall and winter. After months of work, he was able to prove that, although the ratios of fatty acids within each body change over time, they are essentially the same for every body at comparable points in the decomposition process. In fact, they create a byproduct timeline that he believed could be used to determine how long a body had been decomposing. All he had to do was document the ratios and compare them to ratios from soil under a corpse at a crime scene.

After refining his process, Vass was able to estimate time since death with an accuracy of plus or minus two days for every month of decay. The technique has proved workable even if body fluids are recovered from mattresses, carpeting, clothing, and the like. As a secondary finding, Vass discovered that body fluids can be used to help determine ethnicity of a badly decomposed corpse. Melanin is the pigment that gives skin its dark color; the more melanin a person has, the darker their skin is. It is another recoverable compound that leaches

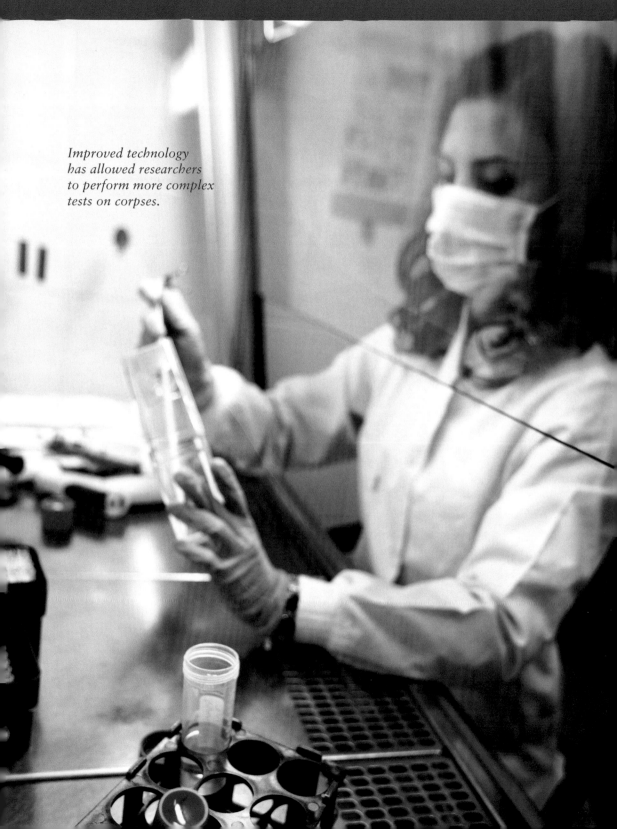

Improved technology has allowed researchers to perform more complex tests on corpses.

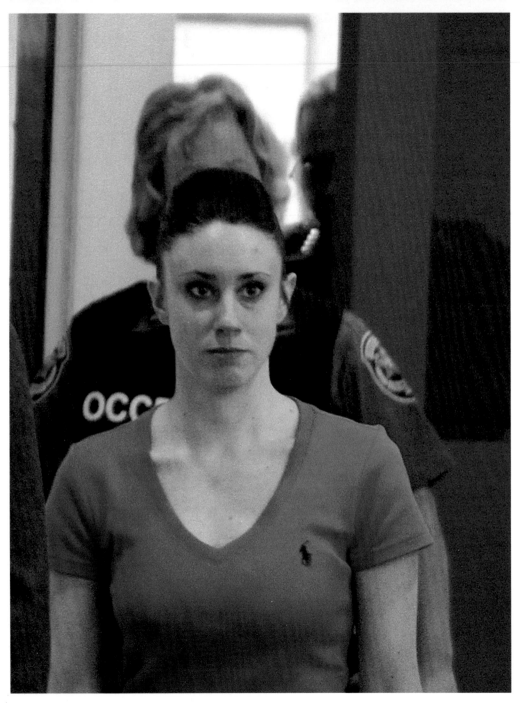

Arpad Vass was asked to use the results of his past research to determine whether Casey Anthony (shown here) had put the body of her daughter Caylee in the trunk of a car.

Problems with Court Cases

There are many reasons why a jury may come to a decision that seems to contradict the evidence. One is that the defendant's lawyers work hard to discredit the evidence and the experts who provide it. For example,

[Casey Anthony's lawyer] tried to suggest Vass had a financial interest in the case, which he denied, and also tried to cast doubt on the testing methods, protocols and quality control. He tried to get Vass to say the fatty acids found ... could have been from [animal] meat, but Vass said it would have had to be raw meat with a high fat percentage and with bacteria normally found in human bodies.[1]

Another reason why a jury may make a certain decision is that juries are made up of regular people who often do not know much about forensic science. They may have difficulty understanding what the expert is trying to say, and they may also be swayed by how guilty or innocent the accused person acts at the trial. In the end, it was determined that Anthony killed her daughter by accident. Retired judge Belvin Perry explained,

"The jury did what the jury did and there are various views as to how this evidence could be perceived," he said. Belvin said there was evidence for a first-degree murder conviction, but it depended on perspective. Looked at through different lenses, he said, the evidence also supported a conviction for second-degree murder or for manslaughter [accidental killing].

Or jurors could have said they didn't know what happened. "Thus, there's a reasonable doubt. We don't know. We don't know translates to not guilty," he said.[2]

Cases such as this one highlight the importance of the body farms' work. The more researchers know about how to interpret evidence, the more clearly they can present it in court to show untrained jurors that someone is guilty beyond a reasonable doubt.

1. Ashley Hayes, "Scientist: Body in Casey Anthony's Trunk 'Only Plausible Explanation,'" CNN, June 6, 2011. www.cnn.com/2011/CRIME/06/06/florida.casey.anthony.trial/index.html.

2. Steve Almasy, "Casey Anthony Judge: She Probably Killed Her Daughter—by Accident," CNN, last updated March 3, 2017. www.cnn.com/2017/03/02/us/casey-anthony-judge-hln/index.html.

from the body during decay. Analysis of byproducts of black subjects yields much higher concentrations of melanin than in white subjects.

Vass's research into body fluids has been used as evidence in murder cases, but sometimes evidence is not enough. In 2011, when 25-year-old Casey Anthony was accused of murdering her 2-year-old daughter Caylee, Vass was called to examine the evidence:

Vass ... said he and his partners have, as part of their general research, identified some 30 compounds as significant in the human decomposition process. Seven of those were confirmed in Anthony's trunk ...

Prosecutor Jeff Ashton asked Vass if, given the test results and his own observations regarding the odor [in Anthony's trunk], he believed a dead body had been in the trunk.

"I can find no other plausible explanation, other than that, to explain all the results we found," Vass said.[55]

Vass also found that in the trunk, the level of chloroform—a drug that can be used to make people fall unconscious—was incredibly high, suggesting that Anthony had caused her daughter to lose consciousness and then put the girl in the trunk of the car. Despite Vass's testimony, Anthony was found not guilty of murder.

Studying Smells

Researchers have also studied the molecular makeup of gases that are released during decomposition. To capture these gases for analysis, freshly dead corpses are buried in graves outfitted with a network of pipes with perforations, or small holes, running below and above each body. The pipes open above ground and are fitted with absorbent carbon traps that collect odor molecules that are generated as the body decomposes. When the contents of the traps are analyzed, around 450 compounds can be identified. Thirty are consistently detectable in all soil types and at all burial depths. Researchers are working to assemble the compounds into a decompositional order analysis computer database, which would be the first step in identifying an "odor signature" unique to human decomposition.

The research has more than one potential forensic application. Identified odor compounds might be used in the training of cadaver dogs, which can sniff out buried or unburied human remains. Currently, trainers use a variety of chemical substitutes that smell similar to a decomposing body, or they carry a container of soil collected from under a corpse. Trainers must be extremely careful when working with this so-called "dirty dirt" so they do not expose themselves to HIV/AIDS, hepatitis, and other diseases

Forensic experts sometimes use cadaver dogs to find corpses.

transmitted through body fluids. Using identified odor compounds would replace this risky method.

Another possible application of odor analysis is the creation of a decomposition detector that can be used to sniff out a body the way a cadaver dog does. The skills and abilities of cadaver dogs make them a respected part of forensic teams; according to *U.S. News & World Report*, they can sniff out bodies buried under 70 feet (21 m) of dirt, and some have found bodies underneath 250 feet (76 m) of water. The North Carolina body farm is best known for its twice-yearly cadaver dog training. However, there are few other training programs in the United States, which limits the number of dogs law enforcement has available. Additionally, even with the best of care, they sometimes suffer from illnesses that affect their sense of smell. They can also become tired, distracted, or discouraged during long-term recovery efforts.

With these problems in mind, researchers hope to one day perfect an electronic nose much like a metal detector that can be passed over the ground to pick up the odors of death; however, as of 2017, experts who work with cadaver dogs still praise the dogs' abilities and say there is no technology that can come close to replacing them.

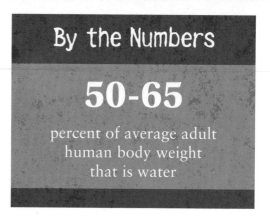

By the Numbers

50-65

percent of average adult human body weight that is water

GPR: A Valuable but Unreliable Tool

There are several types of technology that can scan the ground and return certain kinds of waves to let experts know whether there is anything unusual in the ground. One of these is called ground-penetrating radar (GPR). GPR sends out radar waves, and when the waves hit a buried object or a variation in the soil density, these waves reflect back to an antenna that picks up and records the variations. GPR is sometimes used by volunteers or employees in older cemeteries to find unmarked graves, so law enforcement officials hope they could use it to find hidden graves outside a cemetery.

Intepreting the variations is not easy, however. Sometimes, images that look like bodies are indeed bodies, but other times, the variations can be misleading. Research involving odor technology and GPR was put to a real-life test in February 2008, when a 5-member

GPR (shown here) can sometimes be used to help researchers figure out where bodies are buried. However, it is not a foolproof method.

team of investigators traveled to Barker Ranch in Nevada to search for possible victims of Charles Manson, who started a cult and encouraged his followers to commit multiple murders in the late 1960s. One of the cult members later stated that at least three people had been murdered and buried at Barker Ranch during that time.

The investigative team included Vass, as well as a cadaver dog who alerted the researchers to possible decomposition odors rising from a patch of ground. The investigators then turned to GPR to look for bodies underground at the site. "We're getting the highest hits ... where the ground is soft," stated researcher Marc Wise. "There's definitely something down there. We just can't know yet exactly what until we dig."[56]

Despite all the high-tech signs that human bodies lay underground at Barker Ranch, when four exploratory holes were finally dug in May 2008, no human bones, bodies, or clothing were found. Researchers were left trying to figure out why the dog and machines had so misled them. They finally concluded that native plants at the site produced many of the same chemical compounds they were testing for. In addition, the GPR had apparently bounced off roots and other natural features, such as ant-hills and magnetic rocks, beneath the surface. The failure was disappointing but did not discourage Vass. He stated,

"We're just not there yet. We did the best we could, but this was an exploratory excavation. We're still developing the science, still trying to understand how to work in an environment like this."[57]

The statement expresses body farm researchers' optimistic philosophy. Just as Bass was motivated by the Colonel Shy blunder, new generations push past setbacks to refine techniques, study variables, and identify new methods to help solve crimes.

Using Technology to Find Mass Graves

Another new technology body farm researchers have begun using is called lidar, which "is a remote sensing laser technology that analyzes light reflections to detect subtle changes in the topography of the land."[58] It can be used to find small hills or dips that would be difficult for a person to find with their eyes alone. In 2013, forensic anthropology professor Amy Mundorff began performing experiments at the Knoxville site to find out whether lidar could be used to find mass graves. Mass graves are generally created after a violent event such as the Holocaust or the genocide that occurred in 1995 in Bosnia, a country in eastern Europe. These graves are often unmarked and cannot be found years later. Forensic anthropologists have teamed up with human rights

New Ways to Determine PMI

Scientists throughout the world continue to search for more accurate ways to determine of time of death. In her book *Corpse: Nature, Forensics, and the Struggle to Pinpoint Time of Death*, author Jessica Snyder Sachs explained one technique that shows potential:

> [Researchers] are pioneering entirely new tests for postmortem interval based on such things as the breakdown of nuclear and mitochondrial DNA ... Among the most promising is a test of bioelectrical impedence [resistance] across various parts of a dead body. In essence, such a test measures the speed with which a small electric current passes through tissue ... What pathologists noticed was that in the first twelve to twenty-four hours after death, the natural impedence of any tissue gradually increases, for the simple reason that electricity passes more slowly through colder tissues. After twenty-four hours, impedence drops again as dying cells spill their electrolyte-rich fluid contents. By measuring this deceleration and subsequent acceleration of current through tissue, postmortem tests of impedence become a continuous measure of body cooling (algor mortis) followed by cell destruction (autolysis) that continues for up to seventy-two hours after death.[1]

1. Jessica Snyder Sachs, *Corpse: Nature, Forensics, and the Struggle to Pinpoint Time of Death*. New York, NY: MJF, 2001, pp. 257–258.

groups to find these graves and identify the bodies in them so their families will know what happened and the bodies can be reburied with respect. If the murderers are still alive, researchers may also be able to collect evidence from the graves that can be used to bring them to justice.

Mundorff's experiment involved burying 10 bodies in 1 grave, then documenting changes in the surrounding area. *Mental Floss* explained why lidar was necessary:

If the extra nitrogen emitting from the corpses went into the soil, theoretically it would fertilize plants, resulting in subtle cues over the burial site—the plants would be greener and taller than the surrounding vegetation because they'd thrive in the aerated nitrogen-rich soil. That fine contrast—potentially not discernible [noticeable] by people traveling ... on foot—might be detectable with lidar.[59]

Mundorff and her team also plan to use thermal imaging technology to detect heat below the soil. They believe a grave with multiple bodies in it will give off more heat than a grave with just one body, and they hope their research will prove this theory.

Other Research Projects

The Texas State University body farm has focused its research on using infrared technology and drones. These methods save people time and effort when searching for bodies. An infrared camera detects heat, or infrared energy, and produces an image of where that heat is located in the surrounding area. This is called a heat signature. These cameras can be attached to drones, which can be sent to fly over and photograph an area. The camera would show a decaying body as having a higher heat signature than the plants and dirt around it if it had a lot of stage three maggots on it. Using infrared and drone technology would allow experts to search the Texas desert for people who die trying to cross from Mexico to the United States without exposing searchers to dangerous temperatures.

Meanwhile, the Sam Houston State University body farm is working on

An infrared camera shows the heat signature of an object or creature, which can make it easier for experts to locate bodies.

using 3D scanning on incomplete pelvis bones to get a better idea of an unidentified body's sex. Researchers there are also studying how fire affects a person's skeleton so bones recovered from a fire can be better identified.

At the Southern Illinois University body farm, researchers have published studies on what happens to bodies when they are run over by lawnmowers or buried in concrete. Since many buried bodies are found by accident, often by lawnmowers or construction equipment, the results of that study will help researchers identify which marks on the bones were made by the lawnmower rather than by a murder weapon. Encasing a body in concrete has been shown to preserve it for longer, so if a body is found in that condition, law enforcement teams would know to look at missing persons reports from several years ago rather than several months ago.

Other types of research using new and improved technologies are ongoing at all the body farms in the world, and new body farms are being proposed all the time. Additionally, because of their creativeness and because so much of their work has proven valuable in the field, existing body farm facilities have expanded from research centers to centers of information and education. A growing number of experts ranging from journalists to war crimes investigators take advantage of the knowledge and opportunities found within the privacy fences. "Everybody picks up the phone and calls us when they have questions about decomposing bodies," said researcher Joseph Hefner. "We hear from agencies all over the country."[60]

Chapter Six
The Future of Body Farms

Body farms have come a long way since the 1980s. Today, as they have gained worldwide recognition, they have received more land, more money, and more technology to help them with their research. Many have also expanded to include training programs in other areas of law enforcement. "I'm really surprised that so many people are interested in the Body Farm," Bass stated in 2000. "This was set up because I needed to know what happened to bodies decaying in Tennessee. I never thought [it] would be famous."[61]

Working with the Community

Community outreach was the first offshoot of basic research at the body farm in Tennessee. Bass observed, "Many of my fellow forensic anthropologists—probably nine out of ten—have never worked a crime scene ... They stay clean and dry that way, but they also miss a lot of evidence that could reveal the truth about what happened to a murder victim."[62]

As more body farms are established, forensic response teams—students and faculty who are on call when law enforcement finds a skeleton or decomposing body—continue to be an important part of the research experience. In February 2008, a team from the North Carolina body farm used their skills to retrieve human bones found in a remote area of Nantahala National Forest. The effort was complicated by the fact that hunters had used the spot to dump animal carcasses, so searchers needed to be able to distinguish human bones from animal remains. "They've always dropped whatever they were doing to help us in our investigations," said Brian Leopard of the Macon County, North Carolina, Sheriff's Department. "They help eliminate a lot of false leads. It is a valuable asset to the law enforcement community to have ... this expertise."[63]

As 21st century body farm researchers

practice their skills, many earlier graduates apply what they learned to other careers. More than half of the forensic anthropologists in the United States today trained at the Tennessee facility, but not all of them solve murders.

Although not an alumnus of the Knoxville body farm, forensic anthropologist John Williams, head of the North Carolina facility, is a member of a team of specialists involved in Disaster Mortuary Operational Response Teams, part of the U.S. Department of Health and Human Services. The teams deal with victim identification and mortuary services after mass fatality disasters. Shortly after the terrorist attacks on September 11, 2001, in the United

Being able to tell the difference between human bones and animal bones is an important skill for forensic anthropologists to learn.

Excavating a Grave

In order to collect and document every piece of evidence, crime scene investigators follow a set of steps when excavating a hidden grave:

1. Photograph the grave site before excavation and at each step thereafter.
2. Clear away debris and vegetation to expose disturbed ground.
3. Lay a grid around the perimeter of the grave using string or rope to aid in documenting evidence found in the grave.
4. Remove soil from the grave layer by layer. All soil should be sifted and checked for any evidence that may have been buried with the body.
5. When the body is reached, carefully remove soil from around it by hand or by using small brushes and trowels.
6. Remove remains by hand and package for later identification and analysis. After remains are removed, excavate and examine an additional 6 inches (15 cm) of soil for further evidence such as teeth, small bones, and bullets.

States, Williams spent about two weeks sorting through debris from Ground Zero—the site of the destroyed twin towers of the World Trade Center in New York City. A founding member of the U.S. Department of Homeland Security, Williams also has assisted in the identification of victims of at least two airline crashes.

Other Areas of Expertise

Body farms are not only launching pads for highly skilled and motivated forensic experts; they have also become hands-on classrooms for individuals other than anthropology students. A variety of men and women involved in forensic fields—including medical examiners, police officers, private investigators, forensic dentists, and archaeologists—visit the facilities, where classes are held on topics ranging from locating hidden graves to evidence recovery. Some individuals come from as far away as Europe and Asia to pursue studies that are not available elsewhere.

Some experts visit body farms to learn the fine points of evidence collection and preservation—how to choose a representative sample of insects from a crime scene, for instance, or how to examine and collect soil from under and around a corpse. Federal Bureau of Investigation (FBI) teams visit the Tennessee facility regularly to sharpen their bone-identifying and corpse-collecting skills.

Among the most regular visitors to

One of the skills taught at many body farms is how to collect and examine the soil from around a corpse.

Collecting the Evidence

At the body farm in Tennessee, visiting law enforcement officials are taught techniques to collect trace evidence such as hair, fiber, glass, and dirt particles found at a crime scene. Those techniques include:

- *picking*: Clean forceps can be used to pick up evidence such as fingernails, cigarette butts, and single hairs.
- *lifting*: Tape or sticky paper can be firmly patted or rolled over small carpeted or upholstered areas to lift hairs or other particulate evidence.
- *vacuuming*: A vacuum cleaner equipped with a filter trap can be used to recover evidence from large areas of carpet or flooring.
- *combing*: A clean comb or brush can be used to recover trace evidence from the hair of an individual.
- *clipping*: Clean scissors or fingernail clippers can be used to recover debris from under fingernails.

the body farm in Tennessee are attendees of the National Forensic Academy (NFA). This is a 10-week training program designed to teach law enforcement personnel the best way to recover bodies and process crime scenes. Those who are admitted must show an interest and aptitude for forensic work. They get 400 hours of in-depth training in such varied skills as fingerprinting the dead and calculating time since death.

The Florida body farm is also intended to teach multiple skills. Plans have been drawn for a training facility that would "teach students and professionals in law enforcement and forensics how to prevent and prosecute violent crimes, investigate missing and endangered persons cases, and combat domestic terrorism."[64] The training facility would be open to national as well as local law enforcement officials, and experts believe there is potential for other training facilities to be built in the nearby area.

By the Numbers

4.4

number of murders per 100,000 people in the United States in 2014

Studying Specific Scenarios

In addition to sharpening their skills, law enforcement and others sometimes turn to body farm staff to get answers to specific questions. For instance, the FBI asked the Tennessee facility to research how concealment in the hot trunk of a car affected the decomposition of hair. A group of attorneys suing a Georgia crematorium commissioned a study to find out what a wood-chipping machine does to bone. The Batesville Casket Company requested a study to find out exactly what happens to bodies inside their containers.

Sometimes researchers are asked to set up an experiment to try to answer questions relating to a specific crime. "What we'll do is simulate [reproduce] that scenario … where something doesn't decompose the way it's expected to," said researcher Rebecca Wilson. "Is this natural, or is this because [of] what the perpetrator did?"[65]

Creating More Body Farms

With law enforcement and the public more aware that body farms are invaluable assets to communities, supporters continue to hope that more facilities will continue to be established not only in the United States, but also in other parts of the world. Experts understand the need for body farms that are able to study a wider range of conditions. For example,

researchers still do not know much about how bodies decompose in water. It can be much more difficult to determine the PMI when a body has been sitting in water for a long time; if the water is very deep, the pressure prevents the body from releasing the gases it does on land, and flies cannot lay their eggs on a body underwater. For these reasons, researchers are working on finding different ways to calculate time since death for corpses found in water. They have done experiments with pig corpses, but experiments at the Knoxville site have shown that pigs decompose differently than humans do, so the information may not be entirely accurate. Since Florida is a coastal state and bodies are sometimes found there in a swampy area called the Everglades, the need is especially great. This is one question the directors of the new Florida facility hope they will be able to answer.

Other body farms have been proposed and are still in the planning stages. In May 2017, Governor Rick Snyder of Michigan signed a bill to give Northern Michigan University 2.5 acres (1 ha) of land to create a body farm. Since Michigan gets colder in the winter than most of the areas where the other body farms are located, researchers there intend to concentrate on studying the effects of freezing and thawing on bodies—another area

Bodies are sometimes found in the Everglades (shown here), so it is important for researchers at the Florida body farm to learn more about how bodies decompose in water.

about which researchers still know little. Additionally, researchers at the AFTER facility in Australia are working on creating another Australian body farm. This one would be built in the state of Queensland, which would make it the first body farm ever to be built in the tropics.

In August 2017, several news outlets reported that forensic scientists in the United Kingdom (UK) are working to convince government officials to let them create a body farm. They feel that since the climate in the UK is different than the climate in most parts of the United States, there is a limit to how much British forensic researchers can learn from the body farms in the United States. However, it is currently illegal in the UK for human remains to be used that way, so the law would need to be changed before the body farm can be built. Glyndwr University in Wales currently has a facility that uses pig remains instead of human ones, but once again, studying humans gives far more accurate results.

The more body farms there are in different parts of the world, the more researchers will be able to understand about the way bodies decompose. Bass said, "I'd hope that we could get to the stage that after looking at everything in the body, we could tell you within a half-day how long that individual has been dead ... The ultimate goal [with bones] is to get enough data so you can look at any skeleton and make a 100-percent estimate of the age, sex, race and stature. I think it may come, that it is a possibility. It's a long way down the road, but that's what we're all looking for."[66]

Until that time, researchers tirelessly continue their work, knowing they are helping decipher forensic mysteries, giving names to the nameless, and bringing murderers to justice. They may deal in death, but their work provides hope to many.

Notes

Introduction:
Creepy or Cool?

1. "Forensic Pathologists: The Death Detectives," PBS *Frontline*, February 1, 2011. www.pbs.org/wgbh/pages/frontline/post-mortem/things-to-know/forensic-patholo-gists.html.

2. Quoted in Bill Bass and Jon Jefferson, *Death's Acre: Inside the Legendary Forensic Lab the Body Farm Where the Dead Do Tell Tales*. New York, NY: Berkeley, 2003, p. 119.

3. Quoted in Ken Beck, "Death Becomes Him," *Tennessean*, January 11, 2004.

4. Quoted in R.U. Steinberg, "Listening to the Bones," *Austin Chronicle*, April 4, 2008.

5. Bass and Jefferson, *Death's Acre*, p. 71.

Chapter One:
Learning from a Mistake

6. Bass and Jefferson, *Death's Acre*, pp. 62–63.

7. Bass and Jefferson, *Death's Acre*, p. 63.

8. Bass and Jefferson, *Death's Acre*, p. 67.

9. Quoted in Jessica Snyder Sachs, *Corpse: Nature, Forensics, and the Struggle to Pinpoint Time of Death*. New York, NY: MJF, 2001, p. 64.

10. Bass and Jefferson, *Death's Acre*, p. 67.

11. Quoted in Sachs, *Corpse*, p. 64.

12. Bass and Jefferson, *Death's Acre*, pp. 94–95.

13. Bass and Jefferson, *Death's Acre*, p. 95.

14. Quoted in The Forensic Outreach Team, "6 Surreal Things You May Not Know About Bill Bass," Forensic Outreach, accessed August 3, 2017. forensicout-reach.com/library/6-surreal-

things-you-may-not-know-about-bill-bass/.

15. Bass and Jefferson, *Death's Acre*, p. 96.

16. Bass and Jefferson, *Death's Acre*, p. 97.

17. Quoted in Greg Barrett, "UT Anthropologist Assumes Role of 'Caretaker' for Decaying Humans," (Maryville, TN) *Daily Times*, April 16, 2001.

18. Quoted in Lawrence Buser, "UT Professor Keeps an Eye on the Dead," *Commercial Appeal*, August 22, 1993.

**Chapter Two:
Inside the Body Farms**

19. Quoted in Kathleen Cullinan, "FGCU Wants to Become Leader in Studying Human Remains," *Naples News*, April 4, 2007. m.naplesnews.com/ncws/2007/Apr/04/fgcu_wants_become_leader_studying_human_remains.

20. Quoted in Abigail Goldman, "Bone-Dry Dreams of a Body Farm," *Las Vegas Sun*, March 24, 2008. www.lasvegassun.com/news/2008/mar/24/bone-dry-dreams.

21. Quoted in Leonard Crist, "Plans for YSU Body Farm Bite the Dust," Jambar, April 13, 2006. media.www.thejambar.com/media/storage/paper324/news/2006/04/13/Pageone/Plans.For.Ysu.Body.Farm.Bite.The.Dust-1851464.shtml.

22. Susan Reinhardt, "Recent Government Letter Proved to Me That You Can Candy-Coat Dead Bodies," *Asheville Citizen-Times*, July 25, 2006.

23. Ben Montgomery, "Pasco's 'Body Farm' in Works," *Tampa Bay Times*, March 31, 2017. www.tampabay.com/news/publicsafety/crime/proposed-pasco-county-body-farm-and-forensics-facility-closer to bccoming/2318723.

24. Julie Power, "Australia's First Body Farm: More Than 30 People Offer to Donate Their Corpses," *Sydney Morning Herald*, April 12, 2015. www.smh.com.au/national/

australias-first-body-farm-more-than-30-people-offer-to-donate-their-corpses-20150408-1mgod0.html.

25. Bass and Jefferson, *Death's Acre*, p. 94.

26. Power, "Australia's First Body Farm."

27. Quoted in Diane Martindale, "Bodies of Evidence," *New Scientist*, January 6, 2001, p. 24.

28. Terry Moseley, "(After) Life on the Farm—Former Dump Site Now a Laboratory of Human Flesh," *Chicago Tribune*, April 18, 2000.

29. Bass and Jefferson, *Death's Acre*, p. 105.

30. Quoted in Wanda J. Demarzo, "Dead Body Farm Is a Lively Class for Cops," Florida Division International Association for Identification, February 18, 2004. www.fdiai.org/articles/dead_body_farm_is_a_lively_class.htm.

31. Quoted in Bryn Nelson, "Death Down to a Science/Experiments at 'Body Farm,'" *Newsday*, November 24, 2003.

32. Ally Mutnick, "Texas State Digs Up Forensic Advances from the Grave," *Texas Tribune*, July 25, 2015. www.texastribune.org/2015/07/25/texas-body-farm-research-uses-corpses-solve-crimes/.

33. Caitlin Doughty, "Over My Decomposed Body," *The Order of the Good Death*, February 5, 2012. www.orderofthegooddeath.com/over-my-decomposed-body.

34. Quoted in Todd Dvorak, "Iowa Prof. Seeks Funding for 'Body Farm,'" *USA Today*, November 28, 2005. usatoday30.usatoday.com/tech/science/2005-11-28-iowa-body-farm_x.htm.

35. Quoted in Greg Barrett, "Researchers Lift Clues of Death from a Field of Donated Cadavers," *USA Today*, April 16, 2001. usatoday30.usatoday.com/news/science/2001-04-16-body-farm.htm.

Chapter Three: Making Important Discoveries

36. Quoted in Mike Osborne, "The Body Farm: Unique Forensic Research Facility," *Voice of America*, November 1, 2009. www.voanews.com/a/a-13-2008-05-13-voa39/340230.html.

37. Mutnick, "Texas State Digs Up Forensic Advances from the Grave."

38. Emily Craig, *Teasing Secrets from the Dead: My Investigations at America's Most Infamous Crime Scenes*. New York, NY: Crown, 2004, p. 50.

39. M. Lee Goff, *A Fly for the Prosecution: How Insect Evidence Helps Solve Crimes*. Cambridge, MA: Harvard University Press, 2000, p. 46.

40. Quoted in Claire Sibonney, "Corpse Doctor Provides Glimpse Inside the 'Body Farm,'" Reuters, December 22, 2007. www.reuters.com/article/lifestyleMolt/idUSN2121893120071222.

41. Bass and Jefferson, *Death's Acre*, p. 91.

42. Bass and Jefferson, *Death's Acre*, p. 241.

43. Bass and Jefferson, *Death's Acre*, p. 133.

Chapter Four: Down to the Bone

44. Craig, *Teasing Secrets from the Dead*, p. 44.

45. Quoted in Moseley, "(After) Life on the Farm."

46. Moseley, "(After) Life on the Farm."

47. Bass and Jefferson, *Death's Acre*, p. 136.

48. Craig, *Teasing Secrets from the Dead*, p. 134.

49. Quoted in Lawrence Osborne, "Crime-Scene Forensics—Dead Men Talking," *New York Times Magazine*, December 3, 2000, p. 105.

50. Quoted in "Groundbreaking Science: Bone Diaries," Oak Ridge National Laboratory Review. www.ornl.gov/info/ornlreview/v37_1_04/article_19.shtml.

51. Bill Bass and Jon Jefferson, *Beyond the Body Farm: A Legendary Bone Detective Explores Murders, Mysteries, and the Revolution in Forensic Science*. New York, NY: HarperCollins, 2007, p. 143.

Chapter Five: Technological Advancements

52. Quoted in Darren Dunlap, "The Plot Needs to Thicken," *Knoxville News Sentinel*, January 28, 2007.

53. Arpad A. Vass, "Beyond the Grave: Understanding Human Decomposition," *Microbiology Today*, November 2001, p. 192.

54. Catherine Townsend, "New Forensic Research from the Body Farm Could Change How Medical Examiners Estimate Time of Death," CrimeFeed, January 12, 2017. crimefeed. com/2017/01/27953/.

55. Ashley Hayes, "Scientist: Body in Casey Anthony's Trunk 'Only Plausible Explanation,'" CNN, June 6, 2011. www.cnn.com/2011/ CRIME/06/06/florida.casey. anthony.trial/index.html.

56. Quoted in Juliana Barbassa, "Forensic Testing Suggests Possible Manson Grave Sites," *Ventura County Star*, March 16, 2008.

57. Quoted in Juliana Barbassa, "Questions Remain for Those Touched by Manson Murders," *Ventura County Star*, May 25, 2008.

58. Rene Ebersole, "Welcome to the Body Farm," *Mental Floss*, May 14, 2014. mentalfloss. com/article/56640/welcome- body-farm.

59. Ebersole, "Welcome to the Body Farm."

60. Quoted in Adam Longo, "UT Forensic Anthropology Center Helps Law Enforcement Worldwide," WATE, April 26, 2006. www.wate.com/Global/ story.asp?S=4822442.

Chapter Six:
The Future of Body Farms

61. Quoted in Moseley, "(After) Life on the Farm."
62. Bass and Jefferson, *Death's Acre*, p. 73.
63. Quoted in Western Carolina University, "Forensic Students Search for Clues in Murder," Newswise, February 11, 2008. www.newswise.com/articles/iew/537647.213.52.171.242/forensic_t/inside/news/list_press_release.php?case=58&y=2003.
64. Montgomery, "Pasco's 'Body Farm' in Works."
65. Quoted in Osborne, "The Body Farm: Unique Forensic Research Facility."
66. Quoted in Randy Dotinga, "Professor Needs More Land for Bodies on Corpse Farm," *Wired*, December 12, 2007. www.wired.com/medtech/health/news/2007/12/body_farm.

For More Information

Books

Anniss, Matt. *Cold Cases*. New York, NY: Gareth Stevens Publishing, 2014.
When a crime goes unsolved for many years, it is called a cold case. This book describes how scientists, including forensic anthropologists, work to solve cold cases.

Craig, Emily. *Teasing Secrets from the Dead: My Investigations at America's Most Infamous Crime Scenes*. New York, NY: Crown, 2004.
Emily Craig writes of her experiences studying at the Knoxville body farm and how it helped prepare her for her career as a forensic anthropologist.

Duke, Shirley. *STEAM Jobs in Forensics*. North Mankato, MN: Rourke Educational Media, 2017.
Forensic scientists rely on skills they learned in classes that deal with STEAM subjects to perform many different kinds of jobs. From analyzing evidence to reconstructing a face, forensic scientists must use their knowledge of science, technology, engineering, art,
and math, which are highlighted in this book.

Ford, Jean. *Forensics in American Culture*. Broomall, PA: Mason Crest, 2014.
This book examines America's obsession with crime shows such as *CSI* and discusses how that interest shapes news programs, movies, and more.

Yasuda, Anita, and Allison Bruce. *Forensics: Cool Women Who Investigate*. White River Junction, VT: Nomad Press, 2016.
This book takes a look at the accomplishments of real-life female forensic scientists.

Websites

American Board of Forensic Anthropology (ABFA) (www.theabfa.org)
This website provides information about ABFA board members and officers, the organization's policies and procedures, and information on forensic anthropology programs for students.

Bodies and Bones
(whyfiles.org/192forensic_anthro/
index.html)
Visitors to this website can view
articles and photographs detailing
the practice of forensic anthropology. It also includes links to related
files on forensic science, DNA, fingerprinting, and other
forensic topics.

KidsAhead: Forensics
(kidsahead.com/subjects/3-
forensics)
This website provides articles and
videos about forensic technology
and interesting real-life criminal
justice jobs, as well as games and
hands-on activities students can
do at home, such as creating an
electronic lie detector.

Tour the Body Farm
(www.jeffersonbass.com/tour-the-
body-farm.html)
This website, created by Bill Bass
and Jon Jefferson, features videos
and photos of the Knoxville
body farm.

**University of Tennessee Forensic
Anthropology Center**
(web.utk.edu/~anthrop/index.htm)
The website of the first body farm
includes its mission statement,
details on collections and research
projects, information on body
donations, and answers to fre-
quently asked questions.

Index

Picture Credits

About the Author

Sophie Washburne has been a freelance writer and editor of young adult and adult books for more than 10 years. She travels extensively with her husband, Alan. When they are not traveling, they live in Wales with their cat, Zoe. Sophie enjoys doing crafts and cooking when she has spare time.